TESTIMONY

An Introduction to Christian Doctrine

•

MORTON H. SMITH

GREAT COMMISSION
PUBLICATIONS

Scripture quotations taken from the HOLY BIBLE,
NEW INTERNATIONAL VERSION. Copyright © 1973, 1978, 1984,
International Bible Society.

ISBN 0-934688-25-7

Third printing 1995
Fourth printing 2000

Printed in USA

Published by Great Commission Publications
3640 Windsor Park Drive
Suwanee, GA 30024-3897

Table of Contents

AUTHOR'S NOTE

Let's take a look at what Christians believe. We want to examine the basic teachings of the historic Christian faith by looking first at the foundation of that faith — the Bible, the source of Christian thought. Then we shall study what the Bible teaches about other Christian doctrines.

Our study will help us answer the three great philosophical questions of mankind: Who am I? Where did I come from? Where am I going? We will note carefully what the Bible teaches about God and his plans, particularly the carrying out of his purposes in creation and redemption. We will see what happened to us when we sinned and what God did about that fatal problem through the sending of his son to die for our sins. We will also examine the results of that redemption in our lives in the here and now, as we have become possessors of all God's spiritual blessings (Eph. 1:3), have been given means to grow in our faith and are now called the people of God. We will conclude with a brief look at what the future holds for us.

As a Christian, then, I will be able to answer the great philosophical questions. Who am I? I am a being made in the image of God and redeemed from my sins by the death of Jesus Christ, God's son, and his subsequent resurrection from the dead. Where did I come from? God made me and he remade me through the new birth. Where am I going? I am going to heaven to spend eternity with my God and his Christ, my Redeemer.

It is the prayer of the author that as you study this material you may be drawn closer to God and grow in your understanding of the gospel. This overview is intended to whet the appetite of the reader so that he or she will go on to further study in pursuit of greater knowledge about the various doctrines introduced in this book.

1

THE BIBLE IS GOD'S VERY WORD

Scripture Readings:
Psalm 19; 2 Timothy 3:14-17

The basic difference between most Christians and non-Christians rests in their view of the Bible. Most Reformed and Evangelical Christians believe the Bible is God's very word, his infallible (authoritative) rule of faith and practice. On the other hand, non-Christians believe it to be just another piece of human literature and reject its teaching on how sinful man can have a meaningful relationship with a holy God. Therefore Christians must take the time to understand what the Bible is and why they should believe it in all matters having to do with belief and life.

A true Christian is one who has received Jesus Christ as his or her personal Lord and Savior and looks to him as the ultimate source of authority and information. So we begin our consideration of what Christians should believe about the Bible by examining what Jesus taught about it.

The Teaching of Jesus about the Bible

The Bible Jesus had was what Christians call the Old Testament. By the Jews of his day it was called *the Law, the Prophets, and the Writings,* or *the Scriptures,* or by combinations of these words. Jesus gave us his view of the Bible in these words: "Think not that I came to destroy the law or the prophets: I came not to destroy, but to fulfill. For verily I say unto you, Til heaven and earth pass away, one

7

jot or one tittle shall in no wise pass away from the law, til all things be accomplished" (Matt. 5:17, 18, ASV). Jesus held a high view of Scripture (the Old Testament), affirming that all its teachings are relevant to every age and that all its prophecies will come to pass. To him the whole Bible was absolutely true and could not be broken or disputed (see John 10:35).

We see by his practical use of Scripture that his was not just a theoretical affirmation of doctrine. It was a living-out of his commitment to the Bible as God's very word. He used it against Satan during his temptation; after reading it aloud he applied it to himself in the synagogue at Nazareth; he corrected its misuse by the Pharisees and scribes by interpreting it properly; he taught it in its full authority to his disciples; and he quoted from it while suffering the anguish of hell on the cross. After his resurrection he expounded to his disciples everything that the Bible had prophesied about him and his death and resurrection (see Luke 24:27, 44, 45).

Not only did Jesus demonstrate his own high view of Scripture; he also promised to send the Holy Spirit to his New Testament church to teach the faithful disciples all things and bring to their remembrance all that he himself had taught them (John 14:26). This was a promise that the Spirit would inspire the writing of what we know today as the New Testament.

The Teaching of the Apostles

The apostles held the same high view of the Bible that Jesus did. Peter tells us how the Scriptures came to be: "For prophecy [the Bible] never had its origin in the will of man, but men spoke from God as they were carried along by the Holy Spirit" (2 Pet. 1:21). The verb translated "were carried along" is used of a leaf being carried by the wind. As the leaf has no control over the wind, so with the writers of Scripture. They set down just what the Spirit wanted them to write, and we call that the inspiration of Scripture.

To affirm that the Spirit carried the writers along does not mean that inspiration was a mechanical dictation. Luke indicated that he had researched the various accounts of the life and ministry of Jesus that were then circulating and had written those things down in order in composing his gospel (Luke 1:1-4). This was done under the guidance of the Spirit so that Luke wrote down just what God wanted him to write. Other writers, such as Isaiah and Ezekiel, saw visions which they then described under the inspiration of the Spirit.

Paul said, "All Scripture is God-breathed" (2 Tim. 3:16). He made this assertion about all of the Bible, for in his first letter to Timothy (5:18) Paul had used the term *Scripture* to refer both to a quotation from the law of Moses (Deut. 25:4) and also to a statement made by Luke (10:7). He correlated the two under the term *Scripture*. Peter did the same thing concerning Paul's writings, which he called "Scripture" (see 2 Pet. 3:15, 16). So when Paul made the statement that all Scripture is God-breathed he was referring both to the Old Testament and the New. What he affirmed was that every word of Scripture is a word from God.

We recognize that human authors were used by God in the writing of his word. Not only had he created them and made them what they were, but he used them and their various personalities, gifts and abilities to write down exactly what he wanted. That diversity of vocabulary and style may even be seen in the translations we have today. Because of this all controlling inspiration of God the apostle Paul affirms that all Scripture is God-breathed. The Bible is the very word of God and at the same time the word of men.

The Inerrancy of Scripture

When we say the Bible is both the word of God and the word of man we are not suggesting that the Bible might have errors and inaccuracies in it. The work of the Holy Spirit in inspiration guaranteed that what the human authors wrote was without error in the original documents. In this we follow the example of Jesus (see the discussion above).

In affirming the inerrancy of the Bible we are referring to the original writings as they came from the pens of the authors. Throughout the centuries some copyist errors may have crept into the oldest copies that we now have of the originals. Through the science of textual studies and legitimate textual criticism, however, we have confidence that 999 words out of every 1,000 are accurately rendered from the originals. The uncertain words do not change any vital biblical doctrine. We can have a very high degree of confidence in the Bible as we have it today.

How important is a commitment to the inerrancy of the Bible? If we do not believe the Scriptures to be inerrant we have no assurance that our salvation is secure. For if the Bible has any errors in it, how can we be sure that they are not in the part of Scripture having to do with the doctrine of salvation? Allowance of any errors in the Bible raises questions as to which parts of the Bible are reliable and which are not. If we are to have a dependable revelation we must have an inerrant Scripture. Only then will we have a reliable foundation for all faith and practice.

The Canon of Scripture

How do we know that what we now have in our Bibles is the complete collection of what we need to know to have a meaningful relationship with God? Could some of the books be unnecessary? Could some be missing? The list of inspired, infallible and inerrant books in our Bibles is called "the canon of Scripture." The Holy Spirit not only inspired the canon of Scripture and preserved its authors from error; he also enabled various generations of God's people to recognize the canonical books when they appeared. As these writings were recognized as having come from God they were added to the collection (the canon) that was already present.

The Bible itself gives us examples of this acceptance of its parts by the people of God. Moses had been told to write down the revelation God had given him (Ex. 34:27; see Ex. 24:4), then to put his writings beside the ark of the covenant in the tabernacle (Deut. 31:26). The book of the law of Moses (now actually five books we know as the Pentateuch) was commended by God to Joshua (Josh. 1:7, 8), and he in turn called Israel to obey what was written in it (Josh. 23:6). Joshua wrote down the record of his achievements in the conquest of Canaan (Josh. 24:26), and this record was added to the growing canon of Scripture.

Throughout the Old Testament as books were written under the inspiration of the Holy Spirit (see 2 Pet. 1:21) they were added to the collection of inspired books, so that by the days of Jesus that canon was complete in the thirty-nine books we have today and which the Jews have in their Bibles. None was missing and none was redundant; all together comprised the God-given revelation prior to the coming of Christ.

What was the basis of this recognition? The people of God during some 1,000 years of Hebrew history accepted the writings of men known to be prophets or others inspired by the Holy Spirit. In the same way, during the New Testament period of writing (some fifty years) God led his people to recognize and accept the writings of those who were Christ's apostles (or their representatives), so that by the end of the first century of the Christian era there were twenty-seven books included in the New Testament canon—no more and no less.

In these sixty-six canonical books there are no errors of science or history, and all the teachings about God, Christ, ourselves and how we can have a meaningful relationship together through his salvation are beautifully coordinated. In its totality the canon gives us all we need to know about that salvation relationship both here-and-now and in the eternity to come. (For further details on this topic read R. Laird Harris's *Inspiration and Canonicity of the Bible*, Zondervan Publishing House, Grand Rapids, Michigan, 1957.)

Interpretation of Scripture

The key to knowing what God has said to us in the Bible is learning how to interpret it properly. Historically there have been three major schools of thought on how the Bible should be interpreted. Traditional Roman Catholicism has taught that the church alone can be the interpreter of Scripture and laymen must depend on the clergy to give them its proper meaning; Rationalism has insisted that the human mind is the ultimate authority and sits in judgment over the teachings of the Bible; Reformed and Evangelical Christianity, believing in the priesthood of all believers (1 Pet. 2:9), affirms the right of every Christian to read and interpret Scripture, following the proper rules of hermeneutics (Bible interpretation).

The first and obvious rule of interpreting any literature is to study the words and the grammar being used to see what the author is saying. Even though the Old Testament was written in Hebrew and the New Testament in Greek, careful study of the Bible in one's own native language will enable the serious Bible student to discover the meaning of the words and grammar of any portion of Scripture.

In addition to grammatical interpretation of the text we need to look at the context in which a passage is written. A proper understanding of the context will often throw light on the meaning of a text. The combined study of grammar, words and context is called the grammatico-historical method of interpretation.

Believing that the whole Bible has come from God and that there can be no contradictions in it, we must let Scripture be its own interpreter. This means that we allow those passages that give us a clear teaching on a particular doctrine to clarify the more obscure passages. It does not mean that all passages will be equally easy to understand, but the major doctrines necessary for our salvation and as a guide to our living are indeed clear.

Moses, warning against false prophets, indicated that we are not to accept any doctrine that is contrary to what has been clearly revealed elsewhere in Scripture (see Deut. 13:1-5). The teaching on the Law in the sermon on the mount quotes passages of Scripture from the Old Testament, which Jesus then carefully interpreted; the book of Hebrews interprets several Old Testament passages, which thus become the inspired commentary on those texts. We need to use this rule as we study the Bible and compare Scripture with Scripture, so that we get a biblically balanced teaching on all matters of doctrine.

The final arbiter in cases of controversy regarding doctrinal or ethical matters is the Holy Scripture as illumined by the Holy Spirit to diligently seeking men in the church.

The Place of the Bible in Our Lives

What place should the Bible hold in our lives? It is not enough just to affirm belief in the inspiration, infallibility and inerrancy of Scripture: we should make it our rule for faith and life. One of the great psalms in the Psalter is Psalm 119, in which the psalmist speaks about his attitude toward the word of God. Verse 105 sums up the position we should take: "Your word is a lamp to my feet and a light for my path."

It is true that we have the revelation of God in all of nature around us (Ps. 19:1-7), but though nature shows us the effects of sin it does not show us the way of salvation. It is only in the Bible that we find the account of our fall and its results, and the good news of what God has done in Christ on behalf of sinners.

The Bible is our guide for what we are to believe — our rule of faith; it is also the revelation of God's law, the expression of how we are to live most effectively in this world. It is therefore the only infallible rule of faith and practice.

Finally, it is of primary importance for all of us to make sure that we have embraced Jesus Christ as our personal Lord and Savior as he is revealed in the Bible. The apostle Paul teaches us that the Scriptures are able to make us "wise for salvation through faith in Christ Jesus" (2 Tim. 3:15).

Review Questions

1. Why is Jesus' high view of the Bible important for us? How did he show his commitment to Scripture?
2. What did Peter and Paul have to say about the inspiration of the Bible? Why is that vital to us?
3. Why is the inerrancy of Scripture necessary in order for us to have a reliable Bible?
4. What are some basic principles of Bible interpretation? Why is it necessary to follow them for a proper understanding?
5. In what ways is the Holy Spirit related to the production and preservation of what we know today as Scripture?
6. To whom and to what does the totality of the Bible point? Why?

Discussion Questions

1. What are some implications for a church that does not hold to the inspiration, infallibility and inerrancy of Scripture? Consider the ways in which this church would hold worship services, what the lives of some of its members might look like and what its future might be.

2. Discuss the accusation that Jesus accommodated himself to the unscientific and ignorant perceptions of his society, that he knew better but went along with the views that Moses wrote the Pentateuch, that Isaiah is a unified prophetic book and that Jonah really lived. How would you handle this critical view?

3. Some evangelicals today claim that the inerrancy position is divisive and that we should not fight a major battle over a minor point. How do you react to this statement?

4. Why are there so many different views on baptism, church government and the last things (eschatology)? How can the same Bible teach these many variations if it is inspired and inerrant? Obviously someone must be wrong and someone must be right!

5. Why is it important that the Bible apply to our lives as well as our beliefs? Isn't it enough to believe correctly? Why do we also have to do all the things that the Bible tells to do? What difference would it make if we didn't do everything the Bible commands?

2

GOD IS THE MAJESTIC SOVEREIGN

Scripture Readings: Deuteronomy 6:4-9, Isaiah 46:9-11, John 4:19-26

What is God like? Can we describe him or define him? If not, what can we say about him? Can he be discovered and fully known from the natural world around us? As finite creatures we must ultimately acknowledge that it is impossible for us fully to describe, define or know God.

Though we cannot know God completely we can know him truly and intimately, and describe him as he has revealed himself to us. God made man in his own image and likeness (Gen. 1:26, 27) with the ability to come to know him. He has revealed himself to us in his creation, but especially in the Scriptures. According to Romans 1 all men know God, though sinful men now suppress this knowledge in unbelief. In the rebirth God renews us in knowledge of himself.

The revelation of God in nature is only partial and requires the Bible to interpret what we see of him there. The revelation of God in his word is fuller, but only insofar as he wants us to know him. God has provided us with enough data in the Bible, however, to enable us to know him truly and personally through his Son, Jesus Christ. The Scriptures tell us something about the being and personality of God and describe a number of his attributes — characteristics or qualities of God in his essential being as a person.

The Being of God

The Bible opens with the simple statement that God created the heavens and the earth (Gen. 1:1). These opening words immediately confront us with the fact that God exists, and the reality of the natural world around us can be explained only by the biblical teaching that a personal God created all things.

The clearest revelation we have of the existence and being of God is his revelation to Moses of his name, "I am who I am" (Ex. 3:14). This statement is a declaration that God *is;* with him there is no becoming, for he necessarily and eternally *is*. He is "the first and the last," a Hebraism which speaks of his always having been God, without beginning and without ending (Isa. 44:6).

When God revealed his name as "I AM" he was also asserting that he is a person. This revelation of the I AM shows us that God is the ultimate self-conscious being, the very essence of a genuine person.

God shows us his personality (self-consciousness) throughout the Bible. He communicates with his rational creatures as only a personal being can. His personality may also be seen in the various activities ascribed to him such as love, compassion, anger and wrath. He is a rational being capable of self-determination (see John 14:9).

God is also pure spirit. Jesus declared to the Samaritan woman that "God is a Spirit" (John 4:24). This means that God does not have a body like men or any measurable, physical form. Because of this the second commandment forbids us to make any image of him either in actuality or in our imaginations. To be a spirit means that God essentially exists and lives in the spirit dimension, though he has at times chosen to reveal himself in our world. The apostle John stated that "no one has ever seen God" (1:18) and Paul declared, "Now to the King eternal, immortal, invisible, the only God, be honor and glory for ever and ever. Amen" (1 Tim. 1:17).

The Natural Attributes of God

God's natural attributes (also called his "incommunicable" attributes) are characteristics which are naturally his and to which no analogy exists in man's experience or understanding. The ones we want to examine are his infinity, eternity, immutability and immensity (omnipresence).

The Infinity of God

Everything that God is in his essential being is without measure or quantity. All of his perfections are free from limitation and defect (see Ps. 145:3). He is infinite and cannot be measured or contained in any way.

The Eternity of God

With God there is no past or future—only an everlasting present. Moses declared, "From everlasting to everlasting you are God" (Ps. 90:2). This is a revelation of God's eternity. As human beings we have great difficulty in defining eternity, for it is not just endless time. Time had its beginning with creation and so is a part of the created order (Gen. 1:1, John 1:1), but God had eternally existed before that beginning. He is not affected by time.

Both Moses and Peter have affirmed that one day is with the Lord as a thousand years and a thousand years as one day (Ps. 90:4; 2 Pet. 3:8). Taken with the revelation by God of himself as the I AM, this teaches us that God is eternal and not subject to time. John speaks of him as the one "who is, and who was, and who is to come" (Rev. 1:4), and the writer to the Hebrews saw Jesus as "the same yesterday and today and forever" (Heb. 13:8).

Time is not an environment for God, for time is but a part of the created reality while God permeates all of time and all of history. Time and history receive their meaning from God and his presence in them.

The Immutability of God

Because God is eternal he is unchangeable. The creation is constantly changing and no day or season is like another, but God eternally *is*. He does not change (Num. 23:19; 1 Sam. 15:29, Mal. 3:6; Jas. 1:17) but remains constant and forever the same (Ps. 102:25-27, Heb. 1:11, 12).

How then are we to understand those passages that seem to suggest that God changes? For example, he is said to have been grieved that he had made man and would now destroy him from off the face of the earth (Gen. 6:6, 7). The context shows that sin had entered the world after the creation of man, and the development of this sinfulness in the human race had reached the proportion of being unacceptable to God and his holiness (Gen. 6:5, 11, 12). In other words, the change had occurred in the creature, not in the Creator.

We can best understand these apparent changes in God when we see them as changes in relationships, not in the nature of God; the change has taken place in man, and this has brought him into a different relationship with God. Furthermore the seeming changes in God's plans are from the human perspective as we see a timeless God acting in time; his "repentance" must be understood in terms of the *whole* of his unchanging plan for mankind as seen from the human side.

The Immensity of God

How big is God? Just as time is not a mode of God's existence, neither is space able to contain him. Solomon exclaimed, "But will God really dwell on earth? The heavens, even the highest heaven, cannot contain you. How much less this temple I have built!" (1 Kings 8:27). Paul declared, "God . . . is the Lord of heaven and earth and does not live in temples built by hands" (Acts 17:24).

Although God cannot be contained in this universe he is pleased to be present in it, having created heaven as his residence. God's immensity is uncreated, while the space in which he chooses to live and manifest himself was created by him. Where then is God? The Bible teaches that though he is above and beyond his creation he is nonetheless present everywhere. The psalmist realized that he could never get away from God because he was everywhere (Ps. 139:7-10), and God through the prophet declared his omnipresence and immensity (Jer. 23:23-24).

The Moral Attributes of God

God's moral attributes (sometimes called "communicable") are those perfections to which there is some human analogy, howbeit imperfect and limited because God's characteristics are so much higher than ours. We are able to understand them somewhat better because we have had experience with them.

The Omniscience of God

Does God know all things? Certainly, for nothing can be hidden from him. The Bible teaches that "the LORD is a God who knows, and by him deeds are weighed" (1 Sam. 2:3), and the psalmist asks, "Does he who teaches man lack knowledge? The LORD knows the thoughts of man; he knows that they are futile" (Ps. 94:10, 11). Thus the omniscience of God is his knowledge of all things in the universe, including men.

Because God is sovereign and the creator of all there is, he knows all things; he knows the end from the beginning, and because he exists beyond time he knows all things throughout what we call "time." Furthermore he knows what men are thinking in their hearts because he can "see" into them; thus Jesus on numerous occasions demonstrated such omniscience in his dealings with men (see, for example, Mark 2:8 and 12:15).

God himself declared, "For my thoughts are not your thoughts, neither are your ways my ways . . . As the heavens are higher than the earth, so are my ways higher than your ways and my thoughts than your thoughts" (Isa. 55:8, 9). His omniscience enables him to know all things.

The Wisdom of God

Not only does God know all things: he has the capacity of using this knowledge perfectly. This application of knowledge we call "wisdom," and our majestic God is all-wise.

He created the world in wisdom (Ps. 104:24, Prov. 8:22-36, John 1:1-3) and he rules and governs all things according to his wisdom (see 1 Cor. 1:24 with Heb. 1:3). Since Jesus Christ is the manifestation of the very wisdom of God he has become for us "wisdom . . . righteousness, holiness and redemption" (1 Cor. 1:30).

The Truthfulness of God

God himself *is* truth in the absolute sense, for he is the source of all truth and is utterly true and faithful in his revelation and in his promises (see Num. 23:19). As we study the universe around us and discover in it various aspects of truth, we should recognize that all of it has come from God. This attribute of God is closely related to his knowledge and wisdom and is most perfectly seen in Jesus Christ, who affirmed of himself that he is the truth (John 14:6).

The Holiness of God

When Isaiah saw the vision of the Lord in the temple he heard the seraphim calling to one another, "Holy, Holy, Holy is the LORD Almighty; the whole earth is full of his glory" (Is. 6:3). Holiness, which comes from the Hebrew word meaning "to cut" or "to separate," has a twofold meaning in the Bible.

First, holiness refers to God's being separate (apart) from the world and from sin. In other words, it is a reference to the majesty of God — his essential deity — that which distinguishes him as the Creator from the creature. This was one of the great concepts of God for Isaiah, who on numerous occasions in his great prophecy extolled his majesty and his holiness; for example, "For this is what the high and lofty One says — he who lives forever, whose name is holy: 'I live in a high and holy place' " (Isa. 57:15).

John, who was given the great privilege of seeing the throne of God in heaven, spoke of him in similar fashion: "Who will not fear you, O Lord, and bring glory to your name? For you alone are holy" (Rev. 15:4).

Second, holiness also conveys the idea of purity. We find this often in Scripture: "I am the LORD your God; consecrate yourselves and be holy, because I am holy" (Lev. 11:44; see also Lev. 19:2; 20:7, Hab. 1:13). Peter stated the same truth in the New Testament: "But just as he who called you is holy, so be holy in all you do; for it is written, 'Be holy, because I am holy' " (1 Pet. 1:15, 16).

The idea of separation (apartness) is still found in this moral use of the concept as addressed to men, for God as holy is separate from all sin and impurity, from all that is inconsistent with his nature. His majesty and his purity are inextricably linked together; thus it is both his majesty and his purity that the seraphim extol in Isaiah's vision (see Isa. 6:3).

The Righteousness of God

Closely related to the holiness of God is his righteousness, which causes him to act in accordance with his holiness (see Pss. 89:14; 145:17). This means that he always acts in perfect justice and in harmony with his holiness. The prophet declared, "You are always righteous, O LORD, when I bring a case before you. Yet I would speak with you about your justice" (Jer. 12:1). The righteousness of God is most clearly seen in the gospel of the Lord Jesus Christ and expounded in greatest detail in the book of Romans.

The heartbeat of the doctrine of justification by faith is the imputation to us of the righteousness of God in Christ. Because God is righteous our sins are forgiven on the basis of their having been borne by Jesus Christ, the Righteous One.

The Love of God

The apostle John made that most wonderful declaration, "God is love" (1 John 4:8). The kind of love that John reveals here is not some vague feeling of benevolence but the sacrificial love of God for sinners. "Herein is love, not that we loved God, but that he loved us, and sent his Son to be the propitiation for our sins" (1 John 4:10, ASV; see also the well-known John 3:16 on this topic).

Since God alone is absolute perfection, he loves himself with a satisfied love. The object of his love, in turn, is the absolute perfection and goodness of his own being. This becomes more understandable to us when we remember that he exists as three persons, who contemplate one another within the Godhead with an eternal love.

In addition to this love within the Godhead we see in Scripture a love that God has toward that which is outside of himself and distinct from his being. One aspect of his love is his satisfaction with his creation: "The glory of the LORD shall endure forever; the LORD shall rejoice in his works" (Ps. 104:31, KJV). "God saw all that he had made, and it was very good" (Gen. 1:31).

Another aspect of his love is that which he extends to undeserving sinners. Man had deliberately fallen into sin and violated the holiness of God, yet the Bible says that he loves us. This love is seen in his grace and mercy to rebellious sinners; it is his sovereign good pleasure to move in a saving way toward sinful, hell-deserving creatures. This is the love of which John writes, "Herein was the love of God manifested in us, that God sent his only begotten Son into the world that we might live through him. Herein is love, not that we loved God, but that he loved us, and sent his Son to be the propitiation for our sins" (1 John 4:9, 10, ASV).

This love is not essential to his nature but is the consequence of his sovereign will, the free exercise of his unsearchable riches in grace.

A number of other attributes are inextricably linked with his love, namely: his grace, mercy, longsuffering and faithfulness. God's grace is his goodness to those who do not deserve it (see Rom. 3:24); his mercy is his love shown to those who are in misery and distress (see Rom. 9:18, Eph. 2:4, 5); his longsuffering is his patience in enduring evil and in postponing deserved judgment on sinners (see Rom. 2:4); his faithfulness is his goodness in keeping his promises to his covenant people (see 2 Tim. 2:13).

The Holy Trinity

One of the most remarkable revelations about God in Scripture is the fact that he exists in three persons. Though God is eternally triune it is seen most clearly in the life and ministry of Jesus and in the writings of the apostles. At the baptism of Jesus all three persons are clearly revealed — Jesus being baptized, the Father speaking from heaven and the Spirit descending on Jesus in the form of a dove.

Jesus' teachings in the upper-room discourse (John 13-16) shows the deity of Father, Son and Spirit; and the baptismal formula in the Great Commission shows the separate individuals and also the oneness and equality of the three persons (see Matt. 28:19). Furthermore a careful study of the Scriptures will show that each attribute is seen to be a characteristic of each person of the Trinity. Omniscience, for example, is shown to belong to the Father (Jer. 17:10), the Son (Rev. 2:23) and the Spirit (1 Cor. 2:11).

Human illustrations cannot adequately show what the Trinity is like, but they can help us to understand certain aspects of the doctrine. One illustration of three in one is that of an equilateral triangle, a geometric figure with three equal sides. Another may be seen in the fact that the elements of the earth can exist in one of three different modes: at certain temperatures they are solid, at other temperatures liquid, and if heated sufficiently they change to a gas. Water, for example, may be ice or liquid or steam — all three are defined by the formula H_2O, are composed of the same substance and have the same chemical qualities. The three persons of the Godhead are not just three different modes of divine existence. They all eternally exist as one God.

The Bible teaches that there is no subordination of any of the persons of the Godhead — they are the same in substance and equal in power and glory. However, we do find a voluntary subordination in the carrying out of their activities with respect to creation and redemption. We find this in the coming of the second person of the Trinity to do the will of the Father and in the sending of the Spirit by both the Father and the Son. In essence, however, each person is fully God.

Review Questions

1. How would you define God?
2. How fully can we know God?
3. What are some of God's natural attributes? What do they mean to you personally?
4. What are some of God's moral attributes? What do they mean to you personally?
5. How would you demonstrate the doctrine of the Trinity to a Jehovah's Witness?

Discussion Questions

1. What does the creation tell us about God and his attributes?
2. How would you explain God's natural attributes to another person? Why do you think some theologians have called them "incommunicable"?
3. How would you explain God's moral attributes to another person? Why do you think some theologians have called them "communicable"?
4. Draw an equilateral triangle and label the angles with the names of the persons of the Trinity. How would

you label the lines between the angles to show the relationship between the persons?

5. Develop a list of Bible passages to demonstrate the deity of Christ and the deity and personality of the Holy Spirit. Do so with the purpose of demonstrating the Trinity to a Muslim or some other non-trinitarian.

3

GOD IS IN CONTROL OF ALL THINGS

Scripture Reading: Ephesians 1:1-4

As we have seen in the previous chapter, our God is a majestic sovereign and just to begin thinking about his greatness stretches our minds. We have studied his omniscience and verified from Scripture that he knows all things. If God is in control of all things and knows the end from the beginning, then we must conclude that he has planned and purposed all things that come to pass.

The idea that God has already foreordained everything that occurs in the universe raises some serious questions in our minds. Does this mean that there is no freedom for his creatures, particularly for man? If this be so, then why should we try to please him? Why bother about salvation if he has already determined who is going to be saved? Why evangelize? If those who are going to be saved have already been predetermined, then if I am to be saved, I will be; if not, I won't be. Why bother to listen to the gospel? Why bother to preach it?

These and many similar questions may arise to perplex us as we think about God. We should point out, however, that *not* to have a God who controls all things and knows all things would ultimately be far more disturbing. We would then have no certainty or assurance about the future, about redemption and about eternal life. We may have some intellectual problems with the biblical teaching of an absolutely sovereign God, but any alternative to it undercuts all possibility of any meaning in life or reality.

We need to examine carefully the Bible's teaching about a sovereign God and his decrees. In the limited space we have we can study only a few Scripture passages and only some of the implications of this doctrine. This brief exposure however will show us that the subject is found in the very warp and woof of Scripture. The Bible clearly reveals a God who plans everything and who sovereignly carries out his plans for his glory and for the good of all concerned.

At this point we can define the decrees of God as "his eternal purpose, according to the counsel of his will, whereby, for his own glory, he hath foreordained whatsoever comes to pass" (Westminster Shorter Catechism, #7).

The Teaching of Jesus

Since this is a doctrine that some find disturbing let us see what Jesus had to say about it. The Gospels record that Christ as the God-man held firmly to the concept of the absolute sovereignty of God in all things. On one occasion the disciples had just returned from a preaching mission and were rejoicing in the fact that even the demons were subject to them. Jesus also was full of joy and said, "I thank thee, O Father, Lord of heaven and earth, that thou didst hide these things from the wise and understanding, and didst reveal them unto babes: yea, Father; for so it was well-pleasing in thy sight." (Luke 10:21, ASV).

Here we see Jesus stating in his prayer that God reveals the gospel — "these things" — to some and hides it from others. Furthermore, Jesus rejoiced in the Holy Spirit. This means that his rejoicing had the approval and was under the direction of the Spirit. Then Jesus addressed the Father as the Lord of heaven and earth and thanked him for what he had done. The lordship of God — Father, Son and Holy Spirit — may be seen here: God the Father foreordained all things, the Son carried out his plan through his disciples, the Spirit approved and directed what was happening.

Jesus continued in his prayer: "All things have been committed to me by my Father. No one knows who the Son is except the Father, and no one knows who the Father is except the Son and those to whom the Son chooses to reveal him" (Luke 10:22). Jesus not only thanked the Father for hiding the gospel from some and revealing it to others: he also stated that only those to whom the Son *chooses* to reveal the Father will know him. What he is teaching is that God's plan has included the details of who is to receive the gospel and who is not to receive it.

We might pause at this point to remind ourselves that this doctrine does not make God unjust. Had he acted purely out of justice and fairness all of us would have been lost and cast into hell. The amazing thing about this teaching is not that the gospel is hidden from some but that it is revealed to any — an act of pure sovereign grace and according to God's good pleasure.

One time in Sunday school my pastor told a story that illustrates this concept. A visitor was being shown around a Christian school for deaf mutes. In one class he went to

33

the board and wrote, "Why are you like you are, deaf and dumb?" One of the children came up to the board, took the chalk and wrote, "Yea, Father for so it was well-pleasing in thy sight." That child had come to accept the sovereignty of God in his life and was submitting himself to the will of God in his being deaf and dumb (see Rom. 9:20, 21). If all of us could learn this lesson well we would be able to submit more readily to the will of God when trials come upon us.

All Things Work Together for Good

The apostle Paul makes a tremendous statement about the sovereignty and power of God over all things: "And we know that in all things God works for the good of those who love him, who have been called according to his purpose" (Rom. 8:28). This statement is true only if God is truly Lord of heaven and earth — we can have that kind of assurance only if he has control of the future and of our destiny. Paul was absolutely convinced that God was this kind of a God and elaborated on this teaching in detail in the next few chapters (Rom. 9-11).

If we really believe this statement and are convinced that God is working everything for our good, then once something has taken place — good or bad — we can say, "I would not have it any other way." This is a very difficult outlook to achieve, especially when suffering or some other trial comes into our lives. But this is what the apostle meant for us to do when he told us to rejoice in our sufferings (Rom. 5:3). We can rejoice in them only when we know that God is working through them for our good.

Human Responsibility

Once we have discovered from Scripture that God is absolutely sovereign and has a plan that includes all things (Eph. 1:11), the question that immediately comes to mind is whether this doctrine erases all human responsibility. On another occasion when Jesus was teaching on the same subject he made it clear that men have full responsibility for responding to the gospel.

After thanking God for hiding the gospel from some and revealing it to others, Jesus clearly affirmed that God determines absolutely who will and who will not come to receive the gospel (Matt. 11:25-27 and Luke 10:21, 22). Here he asserted again not only the Father's control over all things but also the Son's specific control over who will come to know the Father. It was a declaration of the absolute sovereignty of God in this matter.

In his very next words Jesus addressed men and laid on them the responsibility of receiving the gospel: "Come to me, all you who are weary and burdened, and I will give you rest" (Matt. 11:28). Here as on other occasions in the Gospels we have teaching on the sovereignty of God in the same context as teaching on the responsibility of man. The two truths are aligned side by side (see also Gen. 50:20 and Acts 2:23). Some people find this seeming contradiction totally incomprehensible. How can both of these views be true? How can the Bible teach truths that seem to contradict one another?

Our minds usually tend to take one or the other teaching and press it to its logical conclusions. On the one hand, if God has already decreed who is and who is not to be saved (predestination and election) there is nothing we can do about it — if we are the elect we will be saved, and if we are not we will not be saved. On the other hand, if we overemphasize the teaching on the responsibility of man we have to assume that God cannot already have decreed who is to be saved—everything depends on us and at best God can only foresee what we will decide, with the ultimate decision being in our hands and not his.

The point is that neither of these logical conclusions is what the Bible teaches. We cannot place ourselves above the word of God and decide what it can or cannot say. What we as Christians must do is submit our minds to the clear teaching of the Bible regardless of the intellectual difficulties we may have with a given teaching. We are to believe a particular doctrine simply because the Bible says so. If it seems to contradict another teaching we accept both of them even if we do not understand how to reconcile them. (These seeming contradictions are called "antinomies" and the Bible has a number of them—remember Isaiah 55:8, 9.)

The Secret Things

The words of Moses in Deuteronomy 29:29 caution us against trying to reconcile biblical antinomies: "The secret things belong to the LORD our God, but the things revealed belong to us and to our children forever, that we may follow all the words of this law." Among the secret things revealed in the Bible are the doctrines of God's predestination and election and the responsibility of man. What has not been revealed to us is how both these doctrines can be true or how they can be reconciled. So we are to believe both of them and teach them to our children side

as the Bible does, without being able intellectually to resolve the problems that may arise because of them.

There are other intellectually unresolvable problems in
the Bible. How can the unchangeable God, who prior to
the creation was not a creator, become one without changing? How can a God who is all-glorious be glorified by his
creatures? How can God be both one and three? How can
Christ be both God and man, infinite and unchangeable
in nature and at the same time finite and changing in
nature? How could the Prince of Life die? The answer to
all these questions is that we must accept them by faith
and not by sight (2 Cor. 5:7).

God Is Not the Author of Sin

We have asserted that the Bible teaches that God has
foreordained whatsoever comes to pass (see Isa. 46:9, 10;
48:3, Eph. 1:11). If this is true must not God be the author
of sin? That sin is included in the decree of God is clearly
stated by Peter (Acts 2:23), but this does not mean that he
is the cause or agent of that sinning. The worst sin in all
of history had just taken place — the crucifixion of Jesus
— "by God's set purpose and foreknowledge [foreordina-
tion]". But in the same breath Peter pointed his finger at
mankind and said, "And you, with the help of wicked
men, put him to death by nailing him to the cross."

Peter stated that the death of Christ was clearly foreordained. We see this elsewhere in the way in which God
predicts the details of the crucifixion in the Old Testament
(see Ps. 22, Isa. 52:13-53:12). But the wickedness of the
deed is ascribed to lawless men. In other words, God holds
us accountable for the death of his son. So even though

God foreordained this event he was not the author of the wicked deed. Man was the author of it.

It may be helpful to think of this apparent contradiction in terms of the decree and the execution of the decree. The decree is the plan of God as he devised it and includes everything that is going to happen. The execution of that decree occurs in time and history, and here God may be more (or less) active.

In the case of the proclamation of the gospel to lost sinners, it takes an effectual call by the Holy Spirit to enable man to respond; he gives the sinner a new heart, enabling him to respond to the gospel and receive Jesus Christ as Lord and Savior. Man must do the coming, but he can do so only by the direct intervention of the Holy Spirit.

With regard to sin, God is not active in causing man to sin. All he needs to do is to leave the sinner to his own devices and he will commit acts of sin. This has sometimes been called God's "permissive decree," by which he permits men to do what they want — which of course is to sin. God therefore is not the author of sin.

Furthermore, God *cannot* be the author of sin because of the definition of sin and his own nature. We have already seen that God is absolutely holy and can never be viewed as countenancing sin. Sin by definition is the transgression of the law of God ("lawlessness" — see 1 John 3:4). To suggest that God goes against his own law is to posit a contradiction in his nature. Such a view of God would mean that God is not God.

In addition to these reasonable arguments the Bible explicitly says that God is not the author of sin. "God is light; in him there is no darkness at all" (1 John 1:5). "When tempted, no one should say, 'God is tempting me.' For God cannot be tempted by evil, nor does he tempt anyone" (Jas. 1:13). Again we must simply submit our minds to Scripture and accept what it says even though we may not fully understand it.

Such teaching stretches our minds, and the heart of faith accepts these antinomies, joining in the doxology of praise that Paul raised at the end of his treatment of this whole subject: "Oh, the depth of the riches of the wisdom and knowledge of God! How unsearchable his judgments, and his paths beyond tracing out! Who has known the mind of the Lord? Or who has been his counselor? Who has ever given to God, that God should repay him? For from him and through him and to him are all things. To him be the glory forever! Amen" (Rom. 11:33-36).

Review Questions

1. What was Jesus' teaching about God's election of some and the passing by of others with the gospel?
2. What should our attitude be toward things that happen to us, particularly if they are bad things?
3. What is the teaching of the Bible about the sovereignty of God and the responsibility of man? How would you reconcile these two doctrines?
4. Why is God not the author of sin?
5. What passages of Scripture give us safe guidelines about the antinomies in the Bible and things taught and things not taught therein?

Discussion Questions

1. What kind of world would we live in if God did not have a plan and purpose for it and for everything that comes to pass?
2. Why did God include sin and evil in his plans?
3. Why can we believe in absolute predestination and in absolute human responsibility at the same time? Cite passages of Scripture to support your answer.
4. Can we who believe in predestination also believe in evangelism? Can we believe in the efficacy of prayer if everything has been predestined? Why?
5. How do we sometimes blame God for our sins, shortcomings and failures? Why do we accuse him of causing them?

4

GOD IS THE GREAT CREATOR

Scripture Reading: Genesis 1, 2

Where did I come from? Who made me? Where did the world come from? Did someone make it or has it always been here as we know it today? These and similar questions are asked by every child. They reflect the natural curiosity that we have about our origins. Actually such questions and the answers to them are basic to all of our thinking about the world and life.

As Christians we again go to the Bible for our answers, and the question of origins is immediately satisfied: "In the beginning God created the heavens and the earth" (Gen. 1:1). With this profound yet simple statement a basic view of the world and its meaning is set forth. God has made it all for his own glory (see Pss. 19:1; 72:19, Isa. 43:7). Everything in creation should therefore glorify God. In a sense all of the rest of the Bible is but an expansion on this basic idea.

False Views about Our Origins

The biblical doctrine of creation is the basic dividing line between the Christian view of the world and all non-Christian thought. Different ancient cultures, for example, had a variety of stories on how the world and men originated, and modern man has come up with theories of his own.

Many of these ancient stories have demigods battling one another, with the winner carving up the loser into the creation as we know it. Others have male and female deities who produce other gods who in turn create the world. In many of these myths a whole pantheon of gods and goddesses was developed in order to account for the different aspects of life. For example, a culture would have such deities as a chief god and his wife, a sun god, a moon goddess, a god of war and a goddess of love. Evil in the world, for instance, may be accounted for by such a myth as Pandora's box, or gods being offended by men.

Such attempts at accounting for the beginning of all things did not satisfy the thinking public, for we have found expressions of general skepticism of the myths and legends about origins even in the ancient world. This is reflected in Pilate's question, "What is Truth?".

Modern man has been influenced by the evolutionary hypothesis and "science" and assumes that the universe is there simply through some evolutionary process without any divine maker having been involved. This means that the whole of the universe, including man, must be accounted for on the basis of chance. This theory does not do justice to the evidence of legitimate science and careful examination of the data. It also fails to account for the cause-and-effect relationships that clearly exist between events that take place in the world.

It is truly remarkable that so many modern scientists, who in other areas require demonstrable proof for their conclusions, accept so naively and unthinkingly a hypothesis for the origin and development of the universe whose only basis is chance; because once you allow chance into your system you lose the system. Where chance is present there can be no system, no cause and effect and no reasonable explanations.

The Teaching of the Bible

Only the biblical account of the origin of all things accounts for the world in which we live. The first verse of the Bible is a summary statement of what follows and an introduction to the whole account.

We notice immediately that the existence of God is presupposed. We find no argument or proof for his existence, for this eternally existing God is the source of everything else that exists. The expression *heavens and earth* designates everything. "Heavens" includes all of the stars and galaxies of the universe as well as the invisible heaven in which God and the angels live. "Earth" encompasses all that exists here on our planet.

Having asserted the fact of the Creator and his having created, the rest of the first section (Gen. 1:2-2:3) gives a brief description of the orderly creation of this world. We should take note of the fact that, though the opening statement speaks of the whole universe, the rest of this section is centered on our earth because it is our habitation and the place where we have a relationship with God. This fits the purpose of the Bible, and it is entirely appropriate that the detailed creation account should be about this earth and its inhabitants rather than the whole universe.

The Genesis account continues with a description of the basic elements which God had created but had not yet formed into a habitable world (Gen. 1:2). It is interesting to note that God did not call everything into being in its final form. He certainly could have done so but he chose instead to create through logical stages. Perhaps this was to allow us to see that he is a God of order. In this statement we see the Spirit of God moving on or brooding over the waters. The Holy Spirit was active in the creation, as was the Son (see John 1:1, 2). All three persons of the Godhead participated in the creation.

The first step in the ordering of these basic elements was the command of God for light to come into being (Gen. 1:3-5). This reveals his power, for he simply commands and the light is there. The whole of his creative process may be described as being "by the word of his power" (see Isa. 40:26, Jer. 10:12). The light so created was part of what we know today as the energy scale, which includes far more than just the light that we see. The creative act brought into being this energy scale, including of course the visible light which God distinguishes from darkness.

On the second day of creation God separated the waters and made an expanse (sky) above and left the waters below (Gen. 1:6-8). On the third day he made the dry land and vegetation (Gen. 1:9-13). These first three days account for what may be called the environments in which various living creatures of this earth exist. The last three days parallel the first three in that the inhabitants of each of the respective environments were created in an order corresponding to the creation of the environments.

The fourth day is parallel to the first: in it the sun, moon and stars were created to give their respective light (Gen. 1:14-19). We must confess that we cannot fully comprehend light existing without its having come from some source, but this comes from our perspective of what things are like now. We live in a universe that has been fully created and ordered and so have no experience of things as they existed in the process of creation. We must simply acknowledge our inability to understand fully how the creation took place and accept it on the basis of the word of God.

The fifth day parallels the second and records the creation of birds and fish, who inhabit the environments of the sky and the seas (Gen. 1:20-23). The sixth day parallels the third and records the creation of the inhabitants of the dry land (Gen. 1:24-31) that was created on the third day. We see in Moses's account an orderly progression of three days preparing the several environments, then three days of creation of the inhabitants of these environments.

Admittedly problems remain here for us, especially with regard to time and manner; yet there is clear evidence of the hand of an orderly God. We may never resolve all of our difficulties to everyone's satisfaction, but suffice it to say that God is portrayed in this account as being directly involved step by step in the creation of the world and everything in it.

The Length of the Creation Days

The biblical record states that the creation occurred in six days, and then God rested on the seventh day. Though many Christians believe that the best understanding of this account is to accept the six days as literal twenty-four-hour days, we must admit that the Bible does not give us sufficient data to be absolutely dogmatic about it. The word *day* is used in several different ways in the creation account itself.

First, it is used to distinguish light from darkness, as day and night (Gen. 1:5). Second, it is used in the very same verse of the period of time described by the phrase "And there was evening, and there was morning — the first day." This presumably includes both the night and the day. Third, the word describes the whole week of creation: "These are the generations of the heavens and of the earth when they were created, in the day that the LORD God made the earth and the heavens" (Gen. 2:4, KJV).

We see these three usages of the word *day* in the first two chapters of Genesis. Moreover Moses and Peter tell us that a day is as a thousand years and a thousand years as a day with God (Ps. 90:4; 2 Pet. 3:8). This variety of uses of the term *day* in Scripture should caution us against insistance on a particular length for the days in the creation account. Orthodox Christians have held to the twenty-four-hour-day interpretation as being the proper understanding of Genesis 1, while other equally orthodox Christians have held to the view that longer periods of time were involved in this account.

The writer has held each position at different stages of his own understanding of the Bible. We should recognize that many sincere Christians differ on the length of the creation days and acknowledge that we do not know enough in this life to be dogmatic about our own views.

The Creation of Man in the Image of God

On the sixth day, in addition to the creation of the animals, we find the account of the creation of man. Here there is a distinct difference in the language of creation. In all the previous creative acts the record stated, "God said, 'Let there be . . . ' " or "Let the land produce . . . " (Gen. 1:3, 6, 24) while in the case of man's creation God said, "Let us make man in our image, in our likeness" (Gen. 1:26). There seems to be a divine consultation within the Godhead before the creation of man. (It should be observed as an aside that the multiplicity of persons in the Godhead is implied in this statement.)

Man was created in the image and likeness of God. What is this image? Some have suggested that it is the soul of man, or that it is his intellect, or that it is his moral nature. The Bible suggests that the *whole* man is to be viewed as being in the image of God. Paul says that man "is the image and glory of God" (1 Cor. 11:7). So man *as man* is in God's image, not just some particular aspect of his nature. On the other hand other passages seem to identify the image of God in man with particular aspects of his nature, namely: true knowledge (Col. 3:10), true righteousness and true holiness (Eph. 4:24).

These more particular aspects speak of some of the higher functions of man as the image-bearer of God that other created beings do not have. Scholars have generally categorized this image of God in man in two ways: first, the image that makes man unique and different from any other creature — that is, his human nature; second, the image that speaks of his moral uprightness before the fall in which he did have true knowledge, righteousness and holiness. Through sin he lost the latter aspect of the image, which has to be renewed in the rebirth and sanctification process (thus Paul's statement in Eph. 4:24 and Col. 3:10). The former aspect (his human nature), though much abused and marred, was not totally lost in the fall — man still remains man and is different even as a sinner from the rest of creation.

The dominion that man has over the world is not itself the image but the result of his being made in the image of God. It is because he is a personal, rational creature that he has been given the position of rule over those creatures which are not so endowed (see Gen. 1:26-28).

The Creation Mandate

The first command God gave to our first parents was "Be fruitful and increase in number; fill the earth and subdue it" (Gen. 1:28). This has sometimes been called the "creation mandate" and is the directive under which all of man's use of the earth may be included. It is the mandate for our study of the world around us, which continues even though such study and use is now marred by the presence of sin in the world.

This mandate also includes man's responsibility under the covenant which God made with him. As originally created, man was in a personal relationship with his maker, which of course implied his allegiance and obedience to God. We may therefore say that man was created to have a covenantal relationship with God, which may be seen more clearly in the covenant concepts revealed and developed later in biblical history.

As a being with whom a covenant had been made, man was to perform three distinct functions. First, he was to be God's spokesman. Adam was given the task of naming the animals, and whatever he called them that is what they were. Later this function would be the office of the prophet, who would be a true spokesman for God.

Second, man was created to have communion with God. It is evident that the Lord met with him and conversed with him regularly, giving him certain commands. After the fall Adam and Eve recognized the sound of his coming and hid themselves, since through sin they had lost the ability to commune with God. This communing and speaking with God finds its counterpart later in the office of the priest, who would represent the needs of the people to God.

The third function is clearly seen in the dominion or rule that God gave to man over all the earth. Man was to subdue the earth and rule it. In other words, he was to be the king under God over the domain that God had given him.

From all of this discussion we see that man was made in the image of God and for the glory of God. He was the recipient of a covenant and was made to have personal communion with his maker. He was to serve God as prophet, priest and king.

We are so familiar with the world and all the things around us that we do not often pause to consider just how great God's creation really is. Our majestic and sovereign God brought everything that now exists into being by simply saying, "Let there be . . . "—and all according to his plan and purpose. Such a God deserves the adoration and worship of his whole creation. "You are worthy, our Lord and God, to receive glory and honor and power, for you created all things, and by your will they were created and have their being" (Rev. 4:11).

To have been created in the image of God is a high privilege indeed. It means that we have been made fit to be ushered into the very presence of God. It also means that our very nature was suitable for the incarnation of the second person of the Trinity, Jesus the God-man, who now sits at the right hand of the throne of God in that nature.

Review Questions

1. Where did original matter come from? What are some man-made theories on the origin of matter?
2. What is the parallelism between the first three and the next three days of creation?
3. What were the purposes of what was created during the fourth, fifth and sixth days of creation?
4. What is so significant about man being made in the image and likeness of God?
5. What should our response be to the covenant responsibilities of the creation mandate? Does it still apply today?

Discussion Questions

1. Why did God create the universe?
2. Why do men argue about how to interpret the days of creation? What should our attitude be toward those who may disagree with us? Why?
3. To what does the image of God refer? What did Paul mean when he said that we are being renewed in true knowledge, true righteousness and true holiness?

4. What are some of the implications of the creation mandate for us today, particularly in such areas as science, family planning and prevention of nuclear war?
5. What should our proper response be to the Creator? How can we show that response to him?

5

SIN AND ITS EFFECTS

Scripture Reading: Genesis 3

"Why do I do bad things?" asks the boy of his father. And the rest of us ask a variety of similar questions. Why is there so much evil around us? How did the world get this way? Why is there so much crime? Why are the rich and privileged prone to be just as criminal as the poor and underprivileged?

Philosophers have many answers for these questions, but none of them really accounts for the universal prevalence of sin and wickedness in the world. Only the Bible accurately tells us why we are like we are.

The ultimate question of where evil came from, however, is one that is not answered in the Bible. Why did the majestic, sovereign and all-powerful God allow sin to enter his good creation? We simply do not know, for on this the Scriptures are silent. We can take a little comfort in the fact that sin did not have its beginning in man but was introduced into this world by Satan, who himself had already fallen into sin and had been cast out of heaven for it (see Rev. 12:9). This mysterious event, occurring as it did in the spirit world, may help explain why we cannot solve the problem of sin's ultimate origin.

The Covenant of Works

Man was originally created good. He was righteous in his nature and inclined to do that which was pleasing to

God, for there was no sinfulness in him at all. He had been made in God's image and likeness, and God declared this crown of his creation to be very good (see Gen. 1:31).

One of the blessings man had been given was freedom —he could choose to do what he wanted to do. With this gift of freedom, however, came the danger of man's possibly making the wrong choice and losing his righteousness. God's glory would evidently be enhanced if his rational creature voluntarily chose to serve him rather than being forced to, like an automaton.

Since man had been created with the capacity for a meaningful relationship with God, a covenant was made with him and he enjoyed personal communion with his maker. As a rational creature it was his duty to serve his Creator and do everything he wanted him to. In order to bring man to a self-conscious choice of serving him freely, God placed him in a probation situation. He designated one of the trees in the Garden of Eden "the tree of the knowledge of good and evil." Man was given the rest of the garden for his own use, but he was reminded of his creaturehood and called upon to obey God by not eating of the fruit of this particular tree.

The test regarding this tree lay in the fact that it was only the command of God that distinguished it from the other trees in the garden. God chose this one tree out of many to confront man with the choice of whether or not he would obey God because he was God. As a rational creature who knew God to be his Creator and who had intimate communion with him, Adam should have had no question about obedience to this command.

This probation is sometimes called the "covenant of works." It is so designated because the privilege of continuing under the blessing of God depended on Adam's works, namely: his obedience. It has also been called the "covenant of life," since this is what was involved if Adam obeyed. If he ate of the forbidden tree he would surely die (Gen. 2:17). On the other hand, if he obeyed God he would continue to live and, after the probationary time was over, gain eternal life.

The Bible also tells us that Adam was not only the natural father of all mankind but also its covenant or federal head. When he acted he did so on our behalf; when he sinned we all sinned in him (see Rom. 5:12-19). We may not like this doctrine of the imputation of Adam's sin when we think of the fall; but, when we consider Christ (the second Adam) acting on our behalf as he died for his covenant people, we rejoice in *his* federal headship and the imputation of his righteousness to us.

Adam, as originally created and the one with whom the first covenant was made, was to serve God as his true spokesman (prophet), his true worshiper (priest) and his true ruler (king). When he fell into sin (Gen. 3:6) he perverted all three of these offices. He became a false interpreter of the world and its reality, and thus a false spokesman; he ceased to worship God truly, thus violating his priestly function; and his dominion over the earth was now corrupted as he sought to exercise his authority for his own glory and not the glory of God.

The Temptation and the Fall

Satan was extremely subtle in his approach to Adam and Eve in order to lure them into sin. He did not make a head-on assault on Adam but came at the pair of them in a most devious way — through Eve. God had identified the prohibited tree to Adam before the creation of Eve (Gen. 2:15-17), so she had not heard the words directly from God but as conveyed prophetically by Adam. The fact that she was removed from the direct command of the Lord in this way may have made her more susceptible to temptation.

We see also that the way Satan phrased his first question to her suggested that it was unreasonable of God to restrict her and Adam from eating of every tree in the garden (Gen. 3:1). In her response Eve indicated that they could eat of the fruit of all the other trees, but when she mentioned the restricted tree she added to God's command. He had originally commanded them not to eat of it but she added "and you must not touch it" (Gen. 3:3). We must be careful not to add to God's word. It has been said that he who today forbids what God permits will tomorrow permit what God forbids. Eve seems to have fallen into this kind of error.

Having first used an indirect approach, Satan now made his frontal assault. He called God a liar when he said, "You will not surely die" (Gen. 3:4). Here we see the crux of the matter as two opposite statements were placed before Eve. God had said that if they ate of this tree they would surely die (Gen 2:17). Satan said that this statement simply was not true, and so faced Eve with a choice between truth and falsehood. When she chose to believe Satan she was following the father of lies (John 8:44).

In addition to calling God a liar Satan went on to deceive Eve as to the effects of her eating the fruit of the forbidden tree: "For God knows that when you eat of it your eyes will be opened, and you will be like God, knowing good and evil" (Gen. 3:5). Paul tells us that Eve was deceived (1 Tim. 2:14) and she took the fruit and ate it; she "also gave some to her husband, who was with her, and he ate it) (Gen. 3:6).

The question has often been asked, When did Eve first sin? Despite her susceptability to the tempter she did not actually break the commandment of God until she ate the forbidden fruit. Sin by biblical definition is the transgression of the law of God (1 John 3:4). The only law that Adam and Eve had was the command not to eat of the tree of the knowledge of good and evil.

Satan had said to Eve that if she ate the forbidden fruit she would obtain knowledge of good and evil. They certainly acquired the knowledge of evil by sinning against God, but they lost the knowledge of good. Had they obeyed God and avoided eating from the tree of the knowledge of good and evil, they would have attained to a true likeness to God in the rejection of evil and the self-conscious choice of good. In other words, it was not necessary for them to sin in order to attain the knowledge of good and evil.

As we read the account of the temptation of Eve we might tend to blame her for our situation. The apostle Paul, however, tells us clearly that it was the disobedience of Adam that brought sin and death into the world (Rom. 5:12-19). It was Adam's deliberate sin and not Eve's being deceived that is cited (see 1 Tim. 2:14).

The Consequences of the Fall

Immediately after their sin Adam and Eve died spiritually. They were filled with a sense of guilt, as seen by their attempt to cover themselves in their shame and then to hide from God (Gen. 3:7, 8).

Before we can comprehend spiritual death we need to understand what is involved in death. Ordinarily we speak of a person as being dead when life has departed from the body. Basic to the idea of death, then, is separation. And so man, who was made for communion and fellowship with God, may be said to be spiritually dead when this communion and fellowship is broken. Sin separates man from God — this is spiritual death. Adam and Eve died the moment they sinned.

The evidence of this broken fellowship may be clearly seen in the interview Adam and Eve had with God after the fall. First, they tried to hide themselves from God, but God sought and found them (Gen. 3:8, 9). Note carefully that *they* did not try to find *him*. Second, the response of both Adam and Eve to God was not one of repentance but of shifting the blame. Adam even tacitly blamed God for giving him the woman who led him into sin (Gen. 3:12).

God then pronounced curses on each of the rebels. The first curse was addressed to the serpent—Satan—in which God announced that he would intervene and break the unholy alliance Eve had made with the devil, and win the victory over him through the seed of the woman (Gen. 3:15). Then God cursed Eve in that area which constituted her as woman, namely: her child bearing, which would be painful. Yet by his grace he tempered this judgment with the promise that she would be able to bear children. The third curse fell on the man in that the ground would now be cursed and he would eat his bread only by the sweat of his brow. This curse also is tempered by God's mercy in that man will be able to sustain life through his labor. Both the man and the woman were also cursed with the certainty of physical death.

These elements of the curse on sin remain with us to this day. Cemeteries all over the world point to the plague of sin on the whole human race. Had our first parents not fallen into sin there would have been no cemeteries and all men would have continued to live forever. Even the creation was upset by sin, for Paul tells us that "the whole creation has been groaning as in the pains of childbirth right up to the present time" (Rom. 8:22).

Not only are we subject to the miseries of this life: we are also subject to the eternal wrath of God. All men, descended from Adam by ordinary generation, sinned in him and so are made liable to all of the penalties resulting from his sin. Every man since the fall of Adam has been born with a sinful nature. That is why David could say, "Behold, I was brought forth in iniquity; And in sin did my mother conceive me" (Ps. 51:5, ASV).

If we continue in that sin we remain in spiritual death and out of communion with God. Thus did Isaiah describe the sinner: "But the wicked are like the tossing sea, which cannot rest, whose waves cast up mire and mud. There is no peace . . . for the wicked" (57:20, 21).

Anyone who dies physically while still dead spiritually goes into an eternity of suffering in hell. Happily, God has provided a remedy for our sins in the person of his son, Jesus Christ, who has met the judicial sanctions of God by dying on the cross as a penalty for all our sins and conquering death by rising again from the dead.

Not only was the human race made subject to the wrath of God by Adam's sin, but the terrible effects of sin were immediately seen in his descendants. Cain, Adam's and Eve's first son, demonstrated the evil within him by the murder of his brother Abel. Then followed the development of sin in the human race as seen in Cain's line (see Gen. 4:16-24). God appears to have been keeping out of the affairs of mankind during this early period of human history, and the ultimate result was the demonstration of the wickedness that pervaded the whole human race and finally brought on the judgment of the flood.

Scripture vividly describes the situation in the days of Noah after the godly line had intermarried with the ungodly line: "The LORD saw how great man's wickedness on the earth had become, and that every inclination of the thoughts of his heart was only evil all the time" (Gen. 6:5). Observe that this passage speaks of the fact that sin had become rooted in the human heart. The depravity that Adam brought upon his posterity was one that involved man's whole nature, so that "the earth was corrupt in God's sight and was full of violence" (Gen. 6:11).

It is striking to note that the reason given after the flood for not sending any more floods was stated in almost the same words as those used to explain the need for the first one. "The LORD . . . said in his heart: 'Never again will I curse the ground because of man, even though every inclination' of his heart is evil from childhood' " (Gen. 8:21).

What is added here is the statement that man's sin is from his childhood — that is, man's sinful nature is inherited. He is born with it, and no amount of punishment or threat of punishment will change it.

What man needs is a new heart. That is why Jesus said to Nicodemus many centuries later, "I tell you the truth, unless a man is born again he cannot see the kingdom of God" (John 3:3). This is the only way the sin problem can be handled and is absolutely necessary for our salvation. We can be thankful that the new birth is part of God's gracious provision in Christ.

Review Questions

1. Did man have some seed of sin in his nature before the fall?
2. When did the first human sin actually take place?
3. Why was Adam's sin and not Eve's the reason for sin and death coming on all men?
4. What was the effect of Adam's sin on his descendants?
5. Why is it that we are all under the curse of sin?
6. What is absolutely necessary for our salvation?

Discussion Questions

1. Where did sin begin?
2. Why did God allow evil in his good creation?
3. How was it possible for a good creature to fall into sin?
4. How did the temptation of Eve compare with temptations we face today? Is there a discernible pattern in these temptations? How do they compare to the temptation of Christ?

5. Why did God let sin and evil go on and on beyond the flood?
6. Is it fair of God to let us inherit our sins from our parents?

6

CHRIST, THE HOPE OF GLORY

Scripture Reading: Philippians 2:5-11

The darkest hour of man's history is now behind us and we must turn to what God did to rescue man from sin, death and hell, for he did not abandon him to his well-deserved condemnation. In place of a swift and inexorable judgment God made a promise that was to become the good news — the gospel — for Adam and Eve and their posterity.

We saw in the last chapter that God announced his intention to undo the victory of Satan through the seed of the woman, who through some kind of bruising would conquer the serpent and his seed (see Gen. 3:15). From this first promise of redemption we learn that God is the one who initiates the plan of salvation. Man because of his sinfulness can never come to God unless God intervenes on his behalf and changes his heart so that he will *want* to turn to God.

In order to save man from his sins and to satisfy his divine justice God inaugurated a plan in eternity (the counsel of peace), reestablished his relationship with man (the covenant of grace), then promised and sent the Savior, his only begotten Son, Jesus Christ, to this earth to accomplish that redemption.

The Counsel of Peace

The initiation of God's redemptive plan began in eternity in what has been called the counsel of peace or the covenant of redemption. God determined from eternity past to save part of the fallen race through Christ; Paul states, "Even as he chose us in him [Christ] before the foundation of the world, that we should be holy and without blemish before him in love" (Eph. 1:4, ASV).

This statement indicates that God has chosen some unto salvation (the elect) and that the saved are to be holy and blameless. He did not choose them because they were already holy and blameless. The next statement continues to tell us about the action of God in eternity: "Having foreordained us unto adoption as sons through Jesus Christ unto himself, according to the good pleasure of his will" (Eph. 1:5, ASV). This tells us that he did not have to save any of the sinful human race but it was his good pleasure to do so. In order to be just, all God had to do was to leave us in our sins. The fact that he chose to save any was only through his amazing grace.

Having decreed to save some, God then made full provision for their salvation. All three persons of the Godhead were and are involved in the plan of salvation, which has been called the counsel of peace and out of which comes the covenant of grace. The Father elects certain ones to be holy and blameless, then sends his only begotten son to achieve their redemption (Eph. 1:6-8).

The Son achieved our redemption by shedding his blood, forgiving our sins and restoring us to a right relationship with God (Eph. 1:7-12). In another letter Paul states that the Son did not look out for his own interests but for those of the elect, for he "made himself nothing, taking the very nature of a servant . . . and humbled himself and became obedient to death — even death on a cross!" (Phil. 2:7, 8). He gained the victory over sin, death and the grave by rising from the dead.

The Holy Spirit was sent by both the Father and the Son to apply to the elect the work that Christ had accomplished on the cross. This he did by effectually calling them, by sealing them (marking them as God's own for eternity) and by guaranteeing to them their eternal inheritance (see Eph. 1:13, 14). All of these actions by the triune God were for the praise of his glory (Eph. 1:6, 12, 14).

The Covenant of Grace

The covenant of grace is the application of the eternal counsel of peace in human history and was first announced right after the fall (see Gen. 3:15). From that point on to the end of Scripture the central message of the Bible is about the Lord Jesus Christ, who is the mediator of that covenant. The covenant of grace may be defined as the promise of God to grant salvation to the elect in Christ. Their response is to be one of faith and obedience.

Many Old Testament prophecies predict the coming into human history of the mediator of the covenant. The New Testament records the fulfillment of many of these messianic prophecies in the events of the first coming of Christ. In this chapter we want to look at only a few passages discussing the person and work of Christ, the mediator of the covenant of grace. In studying the person of Christ we are examining who he was and is; the work of Christ of course has to do with what he did for our salvation.

The Person of Christ

As we examine the person of Christ we find him identified as the only begotten son of God (John 3:16). This shows him to be of the same nature as the Father who sent him, the only unique son of God. We note further that he was already the son of God before he came into this world. The prologue to the Gospel of John reveals Jesus as the eternal Word who is identified as God, and who became flesh and made his dwelling among us (1:1, 2, 14). This is the eternal Son whom the Father sent into the world.

Jesus himself asserted his deity on several occasions. On one occasion he said, "I and the Father are one" (John 10:30). When the Jews of his day accused him of claiming deity for himself he did not deny it. At another time he asserted, "Before Abraham was born, I am" (John 8:58). Here he was assuming the same name by which God had revealed himself to Moses from the burning bush (Ex. 3:14). He accepted the adoration and worship from Thomas that was due only to God: "My Lord and my God!" (John 20:28).

The apostle Paul makes one of the clearest affirmations of the deity of Christ. He uses Greek philosophical language in describing Christ as being "in the form of God" (Phil. 2:6, ASV). In Greek thought everything could be described as to its form and its matter. The form of something is the essence of that thing. The matter is the material of which it is made. For example, the form of a chair is what makes the chair a chair. It is the "chairness" of the chair. The chair may be made of pine, of oak, of aluminum or of plastic. Any of these chairs would still be chairs regardless of its matter. The form, on the other hand, is the essence of the thing. So when Paul affirmed that Jesus Christ was in the form of God, he was declaring that he was God in his essence, thus the NIV's "being in very nature God."

We must affirm just as strongly that Jesus Christ was a man. He was born of a human mother and lived as a genuine human being on the earth. Paul speaks of him as taking "the form of a servant," and being made "in the likeness of men" (Phil. 2:7, ASV). He was subject to all of our infirmities, including death.

In the person of Christ, then, we have one who was and is both God *and* man. He was only one person with two distinct natures, God and man. In the Bible we never find one of his natures addressing the other, for he is one person. Thus we have yet another mystery that we accept by faith — that Jesus is truly God and truly man, yet one person.

Jesus Christ is of course the second person of the Holy Trinity, and as the eternal God he cannot lose that deity nor set it aside. Deity by definition is infinite, eternal and unchangeable. Paul defined his emptying himself by the phrase "taking on the form of a servant"; he did not cease to be God in any way but veiled or covered that deity with his human nature.

In his divine nature Jesus had all the attributes of deity: he was omniscient, omnipresent and omnipotent. In his human nature he was limited to one location geographically and had to grow in knowledge just as we do (Luke 2:52). He was sinless, however, and not subject to errors such as sinners make. His two natures were not mixed or mingled, for they were two distinct natures. He could speak and act from either nature. Since God cannot die it was the human nature of Christ that was subject to suffering and death. Yet, having said this, we must remember that it was the second person of the Godhead who, having assumed human nature, could now die in that nature.

Perhaps we can illustrate the implication of the two natures by realizing that even when he was an infant who had to be held in his mother's arms he was upholding the world by the word of his power (Heb. 1:3). How this can be so is beyond our understanding, but this mystery causes us to join with Thomas and praise and adore him as our Lord and our God.

The Work of Christ

The Greek term *Christ* is a translation of the Hebrew word *Messiah* and means "the Anointed One." This usage gives us a clue as to the work of Christ. He was sent to earth to perform the work of three offices — prophet, priest and king. The priests and kings in the Old Testament were appointed to their tasks through anointing. We saw in an earlier chapter that Adam, as first created, was to carry out the functions of these three offices. However, when he sinned he perverted his responsibilities in all three of these offices. Jesus Christ as the second Adam came to undo what the first Adam had done, so we see him restoring these three offices to what they were originally.

As prophet Jesus was the revealer of God. John spoke of him in that capacity when he called him the Word (John 1:1, 14). Peter reminded the Jews that Moses had prophesied that God would raise up a prophet like Moses (Acts 3:22; see Deut. 18:15). He then identified Jesus as that prophet (Acts 3:17-26). All that Jesus said and did in some way revealed God. In his preaching he functioned as a prophet, for the people testified to his authority as a teacher (Matt. 7:28) and he spoke of himself as the truth (John 14:6). One of the great needs for sinful men was for the truth to be inserted into the world again. This Jesus did as the great prophet.

Jesus also carried out his work as priest. The Hebrew priest was chosen from among the people and was to represent them to God in sacrifices and in prayer (see Heb. 5:1). Jesus Christ, having become one of us, can now represent us to God by offering sacrifices on our behalf and by interceding for us. The writer to the Hebrews makes the point that Jesus was a priest after the order of Melchizedek (Heb. 7). As such he was greater than the order of Aaron, who had to repeat the sacrifices day after day and year after year. Jesus, on the other hand, made just one sacrifice for sin (Heb. 9:26, 28).

The New Testament describes the death of Christ as an offering for sin. For example, "Christ also suffered for sins once, the righteous for the unrighteous, that he might bring us to God" (1 Pet. 3:18, ASV). "But now he has appeared once for all at the end of the ages to do away with sin by the sacrifice of himself" (Heb. 9:26). Thus Christ was at the same time the priest who made the sacrifice and the lamb that was sacrificed. It was through this sacrifice, the death of Jesus on the cross of Calvary, that the penalty for our sins was paid (see 1 Cor. 15:3; Heb. 9:14).

This aspect of the priestly work of Christ has been called the *atonement,* which is the general term used to designate what he accomplished for sinners in his substitutionary work that culminated in his sacrificing himself on Calvary. Christ's atoning work has been described by five terms which individually are full of meaning.

The most inclusive term is *obedience,* for Jesus as priest was totally obedient to the Father in his life and in the giving up his life as a sacrifice for our sins (see Isa. 52:13-53:12 and Phil. 2:8). The second term is *sacrifice* (or *expiation,*) which is the removal of the penalty for our sins by a substitutionary death (see John 1:29 and Heb. 9:28). Next is the term *propitiation,* which shows that God loved the objects of his wrath so much that he gave his own son to the end that he by his blood should make provision for the removal of that wrath (see 1 John 4:10). The fourth word is *reconciliation,* which is concerned with the alienation that man brought about through his sin and the removal of it by Christ's death on the cross (see 2 Cor. 5:18, 19). The final term is *redemption,* which views the work of Christ as the removal of the bondage to which sin had consigned us and is best seen in the term *ransom* (see Mark 10:45). These terms taken together summarize for us the priestly sacrificial work of Christ on our behalf.

That this sacrifice was accepted by God is demonstrated to us by the resurrection. It is because Jesus died for us *and rose again* that we can have assurance of forgiveness and the certainty of eternal life (see 1 Cor. 15:54-57; 1 Pet. 1:3).

Jesus continues to be our priest now that he has returned to heaven. He is at the right hand of God making continual intercession for us (Rom. 8:34) and we are encouraged to come boldly to the throne of grace because of the great high priest that we have in Christ Jesus (Heb. 4:14-16). His priestly ministry continues in his intercessory work.

The third office that Christ fulfills as our covenant mediator is that of king. This is his rule over his covenant people (the church) and over all the earth and is best exemplified by the words "Jesus is Lord!" He was born of the royal line of David, acknowledged as Lord by the angels (Luke 2:11) and worshiped by the wise men as king (Matt. 2:2, 11).

John the Baptist's ministry was preparatory for the coming of the king of the kingdom of God (Matt. 3.2), and Jesus' own preaching verified the fact of his kingship (Matt. 4:23, Mark 1:15). It would be the theme of his ministry from beginning to end.

Jesus showed his authority as king on a number of occasions, such as his power over the forces of nature and his repeated expulsion of evil spirits. He often asserted his royal prerogatives also. He claimed to have authority to build his church (Matt. 16:18), and this was in effect a fulfillment of the messianic prophecy that the king-priest would build the temple of the Lord (Zech. 6:12, 13).

Though there are various references to lordship, kingship and the kingdom of God throughout Jesus' earthly ministry, it was not until he had been raised from the dead that he affirmed his full kingship clearly: "All authority in heaven and on earth has been given to me" (Matt. 28:18).

In his ascension Jesus went back to the throne of God where he is now seated at God's right hand as the savior king (Acts 2:33-35). Paul speaks of the totality of his kingship in his great prayer for the Ephesian church as he adds phrase upon phrase to indicate how inclusive his kingship is: "That power is like the working of his mighty strength, which he [God] exerted in Christ when he raised him from the dead and seated him at his right hand in the heavenly realms, far above all rule and authority, power and dominion, and every title that can be given, not only in the present age but also in the one to come. And God placed all things under his feet and appointed him to be head over everything for the church, which is his body, the fullness of him who fills everything in every way" (Eph. 1:19-23).

As we think about who the Lord Jesus Christ was and is — both God and man in two distinct natures and one person forever—we are filled with awe and adoration. As we consider his work on our behalf as the atoning sacrifice for our sins, truly our hearts should be filled with praise and thanksgiving. Eternity itself will not be long enough for us to grasp the depths of that work.

The apostle John had a brief glimpse of heaven in which he saw the twenty-four representatives of the church fall before the Lamb (Jesus) and sing a new song to him: "You are worthy to take the scroll and to open its seals, because you were slain, and with your blood you purchased men for God from every tribe and language and people and nation. You have made them to be a kingdom and priests to serve our God, and they will reign on the earth" (Rev. 5:9, 10). Then the myriads of angels joined in and all sang, "Worthy is the Lamb, who was slain, to receive power and wealth and wisdom and strength and honor and glory and praise!" (Rev. 5:12). Finally the whole creation joined in singing, "To him who sits on the throne and to the Lamb be praise and honor and glory and power, for ever and ever!" (Rev. 5:13).

Review Questions

1. Who is Jesus Christ?
2. What is so important about Jesus being God?
3. What is so important about Jesus being man?
4. How did Christ demonstrate his office of prophet?
5. What are the two functions of a priest? Describe each carefully.
6. How does Jesus function as the messianic king today?

Discussion Questions

1. How would you defend the deity of Christ from the Bible?
2. How would you defend the humanity of Christ from the Bible?
3. What are some of the implications to the church today that Christ is the Prophet?
4. How would you describe the atonement from the Bible? What does the death of Christ mean to you personally?
5. What are some of the implications of Christ's present kingdom to the church today?

7

REGENERATION, CONVERSION AND FAITH

Scripture Reading: Ephesians 2:1-10

God sent his son into this world to accomplish our redemption through his death on the cross of Calvary and his subsequent resurrection from the dead. These were not simply historical events that we remember and continue to celebrate. They constitute the saving work of Christ, the results of which the Holy Spirit will be applying to the lives of people until the consummation.

This chapter has to do with the application of that salvation achieved by Christ to our lives in the here and now. The Philippian jailer asked the question most pointedly: "Men, what must I do to be saved?" (Acts 16:30). Paul and Silas answered, "Believe in the Lord Jesus, and you will be saved — you and your household" (Acts 16:31).

Before we examine the nature of faith (belief) and the prerequisite factor of repentance (together they constitute conversion), let us study that which must precede these two, namely: regeneration (the new birth).

Regeneration — the New Birth

When we studied the fall of Adam and Eve we saw that they sought to hide from God rather than seek him. The descendants of Adam have steadfastly continued this practice, for all men are sinful by nature, and are not inclined to seek God or to do good in any way (Gen. 8:21). All men are born in sin and totally incapable of changing themselves and coming to God (Ps. 51:5, Rom. 3:10-18; 8:7).

Happily the provision of the gospel is not just the historical fact of the death and resurrection of Christ, but also the gift of the Holy Spirit to apply the redemption accomplished by Christ to the elect. Without this ministry of the third person of the Trinity none would seek after God. Paul stated clearly that all men by nature are dead in their trespasses and sins. The only way men who are spiritually dead can be raised to life is through the new birth (regeneration). This is what Jesus said to Nicodemus: "Unless a man is born again, he cannot see the kingdom of God (John 3:3). Only as the Holy Spirit of God imparts spiritual life to sinful men, giving them new hearts, can they respond to the invitation of the gospel, repent of their sins and believe in Christ.

God described his work of regeneration prophetically: "I will give you a new heart and put a new spirit in you; I will remove from you your heart of stone and give you a heart of flesh" (Ezek. 36:26). In a symbolic analogy that has particular meaning today in the medical practice of heart transplants, a dead, lifeless heart is removed from a man and a living heart of flesh is implanted in its place. Spiritually this can only be the work of the Holy Spirit, for we are not able to do this for ourselves.

As long as our hearts are dead we have no desire for God or for his salvation. Jesus' statement to Nicodemus, "You must be born again" (John 3:7), is not an invitation or command but simply a statement of fact. The Bible does not teach us to try and generate our own rebirth — this is the work of God and God alone. Our responsibility is to respond to the command of the gospel to repent and believe in the Lord Jesus Christ as our Lord and Savior.

As we have already studied, God has by his grace determined to save some of the human race from their sins and has elected (chosen) them to salvation in Christ (see Eph. 1:4-6). In order to accomplish this plan he sent his son to die for them, then he and the Son sent the Holy Spirit to apply that redemption to them.

God does this by calling sinners to himself. The outward call is extended to us through the preaching or reading of the word of God, and then the Holy Spirit calls us internally by bringing us to the conviction that we are sinful and need a Savior. As we read and hear the word of God we learn about Jesus and his work and the Spirit enables us to receive that truth. Finally the Spirit enables us to embrace Christ as he is offered to us in the gospel. This enabling comes as a result of the new heart that he gives us. This is why Paul taught that we are saved by grace through faith and not through our own efforts (Eph. 2:8). Salvation from start to finish is a gift from God.

Repentance

The term *conversion* means a change of direction and is made up of two elements — repentance and faith. Repentance is the deliberate turning away from sin, while faith is the active turning to Christ. It has been defined as our hating and forsaking our sins because they are displeasing to God. Godly repentance always involves a proper recognition of the nature of sin. Biblically sin is the transgression of the law of God (1 John 3:4). Sin is not merely a mistake or an error of judgment but a deliberate act of rebellion against God, and it is offensive to him.

Paul speaks of sin as grieving the Holy Spirit (Eph. 4:30). When we realize that our sins actually cause grief to God we should hate them, repent of them and forsake them. Paul exulted in what true repentance produces: "Godly sorrow brings repentance that leads to salvation and leaves no regret, but worldly sorrow brings death" (2 Cor. 7:10). Here we see that sorrow by itself is not enough, for it must be a godly sorrow that produces repentance — the hating and forsaking of sin.

We note further that godly repentance leads to salvation, showing the necessity of repentance for salvation. It includes the recognition and knowledge of sin (see Rom. 3:20), a sense of genuine sorrow for sin (2 Cor. 7:9, 10), a volitional change of purpose and a disposition that seeks pardon and cleansing (Acts 2:38).

The relation of repentance and faith has been likened to the two sides of a coin. We cannot have the coin without both of its sides, heads and tails. Conversion also has two sides — repentance and faith. True saving repentance will include faith in Christ, and true saving faith will include godly repentance.

Saving Faith

Saving faith includes several elements. First, the person must have the intellectual knowledge of certain facts about Christ and his work of salvation (see Rom. 10:17). He must know and understand the biblical data on what Christ has done for him, so the proclamation of the facts about the person and work of Christ are vital in evangelistic preaching. Just having this knowledge, however, is not itself saving faith.

Second, saving faith must include a recognition that the facts of the gospel fit the specific case of the person involved. A sinner may acknowledge that what the Bible teaches about sin and about Christ is true but still not have saving faith. He could have a full knowledge of what the Scriptures reveal and acknowledge that it is true without ever having exercised saving faith.

One of the dangers for those who have been brought up in the Christian church is that they may have only such an intellectual faith. They may be ready to affirm that they believe the Bible to be true and that it provides the only way of salvation, but never exercise saving faith. They have become so familiar with the doctrines of the Christian faith that they have never bothered to make them their very own by a genuine trusting in Christ as Savior.

Saving faith goes beyond intellectual knowledge of the facts and assenting to their validity — it involves personal trust and commitment. As we examine the biblical passages calling for saving faith we find that they use the language of "believe in," "believe on" or "have faith in" Christ as Lord and Savior. This means that a person must not only know who Jesus is and what he has done — not only assent to the fact that he is the only Savior of sinners — but he must also place his full trust in him as his own personal Savior and Lord.

This may seem to be a mystical concept that only those with some particular religious and emotional feelings can generate and have; but the fact is that we all live by this *kind* of trust all the time in this life. We drink our milk, trusting that it is good for us rather than poisonous; we drive over the crest of a hill without slowing down, trusting that there is not an abyss beyond our range of sight; we sit on a chair, trusting that it is strong enough to hold us; we get into an airplane, trusting that it can fly and that the pilot is able to fly it safely. All of these are acts of trusting faith.

In all of the above examples we believe on the basis of whatever knowledge we may have received, and then we commit ourselves in the various ways that have been suggested. It is possible, however, for us to be mistaken about the facts. The milk could be poisoned, the road could be washed away, the chair could collapse under our weight and the airplane could crash. Then in these cases our faith would have been misplaced.

When we come to the object of saving faith in the gospel, however, our faith will never prove to be misplaced, for here we put our trust in the Lord Jesus Christ as our personal savior. He has already demonstrated the truth of his claims—that he is the God-man and that he laid down his life for our sins — by his resurrection from the dead (Rom 1:1-4).

You may say, How can I be sure that Christ rose from the dead? The resurrection was a historical event attested to in the New Testament by many reliable witnesses. There is no satisfactory account for the empty tomb other than that which the angels announced: "He is not here; he has risen!" (Luke 24:6). All other attempts to explain away the empty tomb have proved futile. Jesus Christ has demonstrated that he is indeed the son of God and that he has conquered sin, death, the grave and hell (1 Cor. 15:57). Men are without excuse if they do not embrace him as Lord and Savior.

We need to see Jesus as the all-sufficient savior from sin, to stop trusting in any other means of salvation and to cast ourselves on him as our personal Lord and Savior. We need to accept his death as on our behalf and trust in his shed blood as having paid the penalty for our sins (Rom. 3:25).

As we continue to emphasize the important place that faith has in our salvation we need to guard ourselves against certain errors. First is the idea that faith saves us. It is *Jesus Christ* who saves us: he alone has saved us from our sins. We receive this accomplished salvation by faith. The ground of our salvation rests in Christ—faith is merely the instrument by which we receive the salvation Christ has earned.

When we understand the proper place of faith as only an instrument and not a ground or cause of our salvation, we are further guarded from the error that *we* have merited or earned our salvation by faith. Christ alone has earned our salvation both by his work of obedience and by having paid through his death for our disobedience. Paul speaks clearly and explicitly to this issue when he says that it is only by grace that we have been saved through faith (Eph. 2:8). Grace by definition is the unmerited favor of God, and so anything granted by grace cannot have been earned but was given despite the undeserving character of the recipient.

Furthermore Paul indicated that our salvation is *through* faith which is not of ourselves but a gift from God. This means that, whatever merit one may attach to the act of obedience in faith, it in no way merits salvation since the faith itself has been given to us as a gift (see Phil. 1:29). We understand that the gift of faith comes to us with the gift of a new heart in regeneration.

Having noted the Bible's teaching that faith is a gift of God, we must not fall into the error of thinking that we are to be purely passive in the matter of salvation. God's word calls us to repent and to believe. Here is another mystery — repentance and faith are both gifts of God, yet they are also acts of men. We are incapable of fully understanding how the two concepts fit together.

In the raising of Lazarus from the dead we have an illustration of how they mesh together. He was actually dead (having been in the tomb for three days) so he could not have risen from the dead by his own power. Jesus called Lazarus to come out of the tomb, and in that summons he was given life which he then had to exercise to walk out of the tomb.

There is a similarity between the proclamation of the gospel to men who are dead in sin and the call of Jesus to the dead Lazarus. We call men to repent of their sins and to believe in Jesus as Lord and Savior. They cannot do this in their own strength because they are by nature dead in trespasses and sins. It is only when the Holy Spirit regenerates them that sinners are able to respond to the call to repent of their sins and to believe in Christ. Faith and repentance are evidence of the new birth, not the cause of it.

All of Scripture strongly stresses the responsibility each one of us has to repent of our sins and to trust in Christ for our salvation.

Review Questions

1. How are repentance and faith related to each other? What common term is used to describe both?
2. What does ungodly sorrow work in us?
3. What does godly sorrow work?
4. What is the essential element of saving faith?
5. What should be included in evangelistic preaching or in any other gospel presentation?

Discussion Questions

1. Which comes first, regeneration or faith? Why?
2. Carefully study the passages in the Gospels and in the book of Acts where the gospel invitation is given. What is often included which we have a tendency to leave out?
3. If someone knew and believed all of the orthodox doctrines of the Christian church, would he thereby be saved? Why or why not?
4. How would you explain faith to a person who insists on working for his salvation?
5. What kind of evangelistic invitation should be given to the lost? What elements should it include?

8

JUSTIFICATION AND ADOPTION

Scripture Readings: Romans 3:21-26; 8:15-17

Many people throughout history have asked the question, How can I be right with God? This was the great burning question in the heart of Martin Luther in the early sixteenth century in Germany. For some time he had had a deep sense of sin, that he was lost and that he was going to hell, so he sought to earn his salvation and right standing before God by a variety of means. He gave up the study of law and prepared for the priesthood, then joined a monastic order to try to earn greater merit with God; but none of these accomplishments satisfied his sense of guilt.

In the monastery and in preparation for his teaching Luther began to study the Bible, and in studying Galatians and Romans he discovered this magnificent statement: "The righteous [just] will live by faith" (Rom. 1:17, Gal. 3:11). For a man who had been seeking to save himself by all kinds of good works this was the grandest liberating news he had ever heard. He believed this teaching personally, started teaching it in his classes and in the churches, and the Protestant Reformation came to be. One of its slogans became "Justification by Faith."

This important topic and concept is one of the benefits we receive when we believe in Christ. The man to whom the gospel is being presented may naturally ask, "What are the benefits of repenting of my sins and trusting in Christ as Lord and Savior? What do I get out of it?"

There are two things that must take place when we receive Jesus Christ as Lord and Savior. The first is a judicial act of God which includes justification and adoption. The second is the change in our nature affecting our whole lifestyle, and includes the work of God in sanctification. We examine the first of these acts in this chapter and the second in Chapter 9.

Justification

All too often today modern Christians do not understand what the phrase *justification by faith* means. Since all of us as Christians need to have a better knowledge of the gospel and some among us need to know how to be right with God, we must study this concept carefully.

We commonly use the term *justify* in two basic ways. The accountant uses it to demonstrate that his financial books are balanced. Others of us use the term to affirm the rightness of an action. For example, I may justify my action of shooting a burglar in my home because he might have harmed my family. We call this the demonstrable use of the word. James uses "justify" in this way when he wrote, "Was not Abraham our father justified by works, when he had offered Isaac his son upon the altar?" (Jas. 2:21, KJV). The point is that Abraham demonstrated his relationship with God by his work of obedience in his willingness to sacrifice Isaac. Though we occasionally find this usage of the word in the Bible it is not what the concept basically means.

The other way that we use the term is in the declarative sense—that is, as a judicial declaration. When a defendant in a court case is declared not guilty by either the judge or a jury, he is accepted as righteous before the court and by the law; he may be said to be have been justified.

This is the way Paul used the term when he talked about our being justified by faith. He was telling us that for the sake of Jesus Christ God forgives us our sins, adopts us into his family, gives us eternal life, accepts us into his presence and declares us righteous on the basis of the righteousness of Christ.

It was as Luther studied the letter to the Romans that he discovered the doctrine of justification set forth in a systematic way. In the first three chapters Paul makes a case against all mankind, showing that everyone has sinned and come short of the glory of God (Rom. 3:23). His conclusion is that none of us can be justified by his works, for "by the works of the law shall no flesh be justified in his sight" (Rom. 3:20, ASV). If this is true, how can anyone be right with God?

The answer is in the declaration that sinners are "being justified freely by his grace through the redemption that is in Christ Jesus" (Rom. 3:24, ASV). This certainly is not speaking of our demonstrating our relationship to God through the obedience of good works. Rather it is the idea of our being freely forgiven by the grace of God, being declared righteous by him and on the basis of that declaration being freely accepted as righteous in his sight.

Remember, when something comes to us by the grace of God it comes to the totally undeserving only by the goodness of God. When Paul speaks of this justification being done freely he means that God was under no obligation to save us. He did so out of his mere good pleasure.

The Westminster Shorter Catechism (#33) gives us an excellent definition of this concept: "Justification is an act of God's free grace, wherein he pardoneth all our sins, and accepteth us as righteous in his sight, only for the righteousness of Christ imputed to us, and received by faith alone."

This justification is said to be "through the redemption that is in Christ Jesus" (Rom. 3:24, ASV). Here the apostle is teaching us that, although our salvation is freely given to us, it cost God an awful price — the death of his Son: "whom God set forth to be a propitiation " (vs. 25, ASV).

To propitiate means to appease or conciliate one who is angry. It presupposes God's wrath and displeasure, and its purpose is to remove that displeasure. Many people do not want to admit that God is so offended by their sin that he will pour out his wrath for eternity against the rebellious and unrepentant sinner. The Bible clearly teaches that there will be a great judgment on sin and sinners, and the only way this wrath can be turned aside is for the offended one to be appeased.

The amazing thing about the gospel is that the God who has been offended by our sins still so loved the sinful world that he gave his only begotten son to pay the price of redemption for it. He appeased his own wrath through the death of his beloved son.

The price for appeasing the wrath of God was the shedding of the blood of Christ — that is, his death on the cross. It is this shed blood of Jesus — his death — that the apostle indicates is to be the particular object of our faith (Rom. 3:25). We are to see the death of Christ as having paid the price for our salvation. We must give up trusting in ourselves, in our parents, in our church or in anyone or anything else, and put our trust in the sacrifice of Jesus for our sins. Note how this passage (Rom. 3:21-26) sets forth the point that was made in the previous chapter to the effect that it is Jesus who accomplishes the work of salvation, and faith is the instrument by which we receive it.

The apostle then indicates that the purpose of this plan of salvation by God is to demonstrate his justice (Rom. 3.25). Since Jesus has paid the price for our sins God can be both just and the justifier of sinners who have put their faith in Jesus (Rom. 3:26).

As we review this passage we see that the plan of salvation stems from the grace of God in giving Christ to satisfy divine justice—a gift that is received by faith alone, for the glory of God.

How can God consider us to be righteous? By reckoning (imputing) the righteousness of Christ to us. Not only was Christ's *death* accepted by God for our sins but the *righteousness* of Christ was credited to our account ("imputed"). This is not to say that God *makes* us righteous but rather that he declares to us that we *are* righteous and that he accounts us as being so on the ground of Christ's righteousness. We are made righteous through the process that begins with the new birth, continues throughout our lives through sanctification and culminates in our glorification. We shall consider this topic more fully in the next chapter.

Justification is a declarative act of God. He pardons us and accepts us as righteous, and the ground for this pardon and acceptance is not anything in us — not even our faith — but only the righteousness of Christ and his full satisfaction of the demands of divine justice. Some have thought that faith is the *ground* for our salvation; but this would take away the gracious character of our redemption and give us something of which to boast. Paul makes it abundantly clear that faith itself is a gift of God and salvation is "not by works, so that no one can boast" (Eph. 2:9).

Justification as an act occurs only once (it is not a continuing process) and it is received by faith alone. This faith, however, never stands alone; for if it is a living faith it must produce good works (Jas. 2:17). This will be discussed more fully in the next chapter.

After setting forth the basic teaching on justification, Paul shows it to be a consistent teaching throughout the Bible by demonstrating from the Old Testament that both Abraham and David had been justified by faith and not by works (Rom. 4). He then answers the allegation that such a doctrine would of necessity lead to licentiousness by pointing out how totally contradictory this would be in view of our being united to Christ, which includes our participation with him in his death and resurrection. We are to reckon ourselves to be dead to sin and alive to God (Rom. 6:11).

Adoption

The second judicial act that takes place when we respond to Christ by faith is adoption into what D. James Kennedy calls "the forever family of God." In the ordinary use of the word, adoption occurs when an outsider is received into a family and made a full participant with the natural children of the family. Paul declared that this is exactly what God has done for us: "You received the Spirit of sonship [adoption]. And by him we cry, '*Abba*, Father.' The Spirit himself testifies with our spirit that we are God's children. Now if we are children, then we are heirs—heirs of God and co-heirs with Christ" (Rom. 8:15-17).

Sometimes the tendency is for us to think that if we have been born again we must have been born into the family of God and do not need to be adopted into it. It is true that God has given to us new hearts — and thereby new natures — that make us suitable to be called the children of God. But the legal rights of those who are made heirs of God are conferred by the judicial declaration of adoption.

Both ancient and modern laws governing adoption make the adopted child a mandatory heir. That is, once adopted the child is considered by the law as coequal in every way with the natural-born children of the family. It is interesting to note that, though the civil law allows for the breaking of a marriage by divorce, there is no such provision for breaking an adoption. By analogy our being declared adopted by God should be a great comfort to us in that it assures us that we have, and will always have, all the rights of the children of God.

We find some people in the world today who insist that all people are children of God. This may be a popular viewpoint in the world but it is not what the Bible teaches. When Adam and Eve fell into sin they renounced God as their natural and spiritual father and transferred their allegiance to Satan. This is why Jesus would say to the Jews who opposed him although they too were physical descendants of Abraham, "You belong to your father, the devil" (John 8:44). He certainly did not teach the universal fatherhood of God or the universal brotherhood of man.

Furthermore John clearly noted that Jesus "came to that which was his own, but his own did not receive him. Yet to all who received him, to those who believed in his name, he gave the right to become children of God" (John 1:11, 12). These passages, taken with Romans 8:15-17, indicate that this God-given right is not bestowed indiscriminately upon all men everywhere. It is one of the rich benefits that come to us when we receive Christ as our Lord and Savior.

To affirm that all men are children of God on the ground of creation is to nullify the gospel. It is to say that we really have not lost our relationship with God through sin, that nothing is needed in order for us to have an eternal relationship with God, that all men are going to heaven, that no new birth is required and that no adoption is necessary. These views are contrary to the biblical teaching on the whole topic of how a man can be right before God. Peter clearly stated that before redemption we were *not a people* but through his grace have become "the people of God" (1 Pet. 2:10).

As an aside we might point out that the teaching of the universal fatherhood of God and the brotherhood of man is the "gospel" of liberalism and is absolutely contradictory to the Bible and to historic, orthodox Christianity. It is one of the clearest divisions between truth and error and becomes a way of detecting whether a church today is teaching the word of God or the word of man. If you hear these false teachings declared from your pulpit you need to find another church where the inspired, infallible and inerrant Scripture is believed and taught.

In summary, justification and adoption are judicial, declarative acts. God declares both when by faith we receive Jesus Christ as our personal Lord and Savior. They are not continuing works of God but once-for-all accomplished acts of grace. As we realize that justification and adoption are ours by faith we should be greatly comforted.

Review Questions

1. What is the meaning of justification?
2. What are some of the other ways this term is used today?
3. How does Paul use the term? How does James use it?
4. What is the ground of justification? What is the instrument by which we appropriate justification?
5. Why is adoption an important teaching in the Bible? How do we receive it?
6. Why is adoption necessary?

Discussion Questions

1. Why is justification by faith such an important doctrine and the separating point between truth and error? Why

do men keep asking the question, "How can I be right with God?"

2. What did Paul say about the justification of Abraham and David? Why was this important?
3. In dealing with a person trying to work for his salvation and right standing with God, how would you explain and support from Scripture the doctrine of justification by faith?
4. What does the Bible teach about the fatherhood of God?
5. How do we become children of God? Why couldn't we simply be born into God's family?
6. What is the danger of the popular teaching on the universal fatherhood of God and the brotherhood of man?

9

SANCTIFICATION AND GOOD WORKS

Scripture Readings: Ephesians 2:8-10, Philippians 2:12, 13, Hebrews 12:14

If justification is the beginning of our Christian lives here on earth and glorification is the end of them as we arrive in eternity, then what occurs between justification and glorification? What happens to us after we become Christians? Do we immediately become perfectly holy? Do we stop sinning?

These questions bring us to consideration of a most vital, practical topic — the living of our Christian lives here on earth. It would be very nice if we stopped sinning once we became Christians, but this is simply not the case. Some Christians and some theological systems believe that we can attain to a certain kind of perfection; but when we compare ourselves to the holiness of God we must acknowledge that in this life we will never be as holy as he is, nor do the Scriptures teach a sinless perfection in this life (more on that later).

Peter tells us to *grow* in grace (2 Pet. 3:18), and this command implies that we do not jump immediately into a state of total sanctification (holiness). It is something into which we must grow daily, and it is an exciting adventure to do so with the help of God's grace.

An early heresy in the Christian church was that of antinomianism, which was and still is a rather commonly held error. It maintains that a person can receive Christ as Savior without that God-given salvation affecting his daily life. Now it is perfectly true that salvation comes by faith in Christ alone, and no amount of good works can add anything to it; but saving faith is a living faith, for faith without works is dead. We are justified by faith alone, but faith never stands alone: it must result in good works in the life of the believer.

If good works and spiritual growth are not present, the person who thinks he is saved but there has been no change in his life needs to reexamine the Scriptures and his own heart to see whether or not he has ever truly put his trust in Christ. A person who claims to have received Jesus as Lord and Savior but who is unaffected in daily living by what Christ has done on his behalf certainly has not embraced Christ savingly.

The Bible does not teach that sanctification is optional for the Christian: it is the natural and necessary result of regeneration and justification. Any lack of spiritual growth should alert a professing Christian to the deadness of his heart and perhaps to his unsaved state.

The Process of Sanctification

The term we use for Christian growth is *sanctification*. Like *justification* it is a word that needs to be defined. *Sanctification* and *holiness* are essentially synonymous terms, both coming from the same Hebrew and Greek words, whose root meaning is that of setting apart. Something that is sanctified, then, is something that is set apart. For example, Hebrew priests (Ex. 19:22) and the furniture of the tabernacle were sanctified or set apart for the special use of the sanctuary worship (Ex. 40:10-13), and so were designated "holy." These meanings do not necessarily carry any connotation of moral perfection.

In the discussion on the holiness of God in Chapter 2 we noted that this idea of separation is true of God in his apartness from his creation. The same biblical terms describe that which is morally good and upright, and it is this latter usage that is especially in view when we study the Bible's teaching about our sanctification.

Once again the Westminster Shorter Catechism (#35) has an excellent definition: "Sanctification is the work of God's free grace, whereby we are renewed in the whole man after the image of God, and are enabled more and more to die unto sin, and live unto righteousness."

There is a sense however in which all those who are saved are set apart from the world and become the people of God; thus both Old Testament Israel and the New Testament church are called "a holy nation" (Ex. 19:6; 1 Pet. 2:9). When we use the word this way we are speaking of sanctification as a *status*, for the *state* of believers has changed: these former unbelievers now belong to the one true and holy God (see 1 Pet. 2:10). This elevation to a new status is an act that takes place once at the time of our embracing Christ. (It has also been called "definitive sanctification.")

The required growth in holiness, however, is a process (also called "progressive sanctification") which begins at regeneration and continues throughout our lives here on earth. The new heart implanted in us makes us a new creation (2 Cor. 5:17) and gives us new desires, new hopes and a new direction in life. As we live our Christian lives with a new heart under the lordship of Christ and by the direction of the gracious Holy Spirit, we seek more and more to do the will of God.

We cannot attain complete sanctification and perfection in this life because of the remnants of sin in our natures. We find that, when we would do good, sin is still present within us (see Rom. 7:21) and even our best deeds are marred by the imperfections caused by those residing sins. This does not mean that we should lower the standard toward which we are to strive, for God himself has set that standard for his people in all generations. It is nothing less than perfection for he is perfect himself (see Gen. 17:1, Matt. 5:48) and his kind of perfection involves our heart attitudes as well as our external acts.

Perfectionist Views on Sanctification

Throughout the history of the church there have been various movements and theologies which have suggested that perfection is attainable. The only way that this kind of perfection is achievable is by lowering the standard of God's perfection. One common view suggests that we can progress to the point where we no longer commit any known sins. This of course externalizes sin by ruling out sinful thoughts and desires. Such a lowered view of perfection makes it seem attainable but it is not the kind of perfection God demands.

Another error that has crept into the church regarding sanctification is that it can be attained by a single act of faith, commitment or decision just as justification was. It has been suggested that, just as we received Christ as Savior by a single act of faith, so now we can receive victory over all sin by accepting him as Lord of our lives. This viewpoint has great appeal in calling Christians to commit themselves afresh to Christ for victory, but this is not the correct understanding of what the Bible teaches about sanctification.

From this idea of instant sanctification a teaching developed that we should not strive for holiness or godliness but should "let go and let God" do the living in us. This approach is also very appealing; for it suggests that, since the Spirit resides in us, all we need to do for godly living is to turn ourselves over to him and stop trying to live a holy life on our own. In fact this position teaches that we should not even attempt to obey the law any more. Although this viewpoint has some elements of truth in it, it is not what God has provided for his people.

The Biblical Teaching on Sanctification

Let us now examine what the Bible teaches on this important subject. First, the Bible does not teach that there are two stages in receiving Christ. When we receive Jesus as Savior we receive him as Lord at the same time, for he is the *Lord* Jesus Christ. Peter in his first preaching of the gospel after the ascension of Jesus declared, "Therefore let all Israel be assured of this: God has made this Jesus, whom you crucified, both Lord and Christ" (Acts 2:36). Nowhere does Scripture teach that we are to receive him a second time as Lord.

Second, the Bible talks about sanctification as being a work in which the believers are to be active, for we are given divine commands to "put off" and "put on" (see Eph. 4:25-32, Col. 3:5-17). Sanctification is not something we receive in a single moment; we are called to obey the word of God, to present our bodies as living sacrifices, not to be conformed to the world and to be transformed by the renewing of our minds (Rom. 12:1). The New Testament has many imperatives (verbs of command) that call us to a *way of life,* not to a single act.

The language of "putting off" or "putting to death" has historically been called "mortifying the old man" (see Rom. 8:13), while the commands to "put on" and "clothe yourself" are seen as part of the "quickening of the new man" (see Rom. 6:4, 5, Col. 2:12; 3:1, 3).

The Author and Agent of Sanctification

The issue of who is the author of sanctification may help us clarify the matter of whether we should be striving for holiness. The apostle Paul made this declaration: "Therefore, my dear friends . . . continue to work out your salvation with fear and trembling." He then gave this explanation: "For it is God who works in you to will and to act according to his good pleasure" (Phil. 2:12, 13).

As we analyze this interesting passage we see that God is the author of the sanctification process since it is he who works in us and causes us to will and to act. Taken by itself this clause might lead us to believe that we are not to do anything about our godliness and holiness but simply leave it in God's hands. This is not what the apostle said, however, for he began with a command to work out our salvation. It is a present-tense imperative which calls for continuous action.

We must read this passage carefully, for it might give the impression to some that we are to work *for* our salvation. We have already noted that no man will be justified by his works (Rom. 3:20). Then what is Paul saying here? He is commanding us to work out the potential of our freely received salvation. In other words, now that we are saved we are to work out in our lives the salvation which we have so freely received by God's grace. This command has to do with our sanctification.

Note that the command is for us to *do* it. It does not state that we are *not* to strive for holiness because God is the one who wills and does through us. Rather it teaches that we are to strive for holiness with the encouragement that God is the one enabling us to will and to act the way we should. On the basis of this passage we may say that God is the author of sanctification and that man is the agent of it. It is like the resurrection of Lazarus: Jesus commanded him to come out of the tomb but Lazarus had to respond, doing so only with the help of God. So it is with our sanctification and the doing of good works.

The Law of God As Our Standard

The only standard by which we are to determine what are good works is the word of God, particularly the law of God as set forth in the Ten Commandments (Ex. 20:1-17). This is the code of ethics given to us by God through Moses, telling us how he would have us live our daily lives. Jesus in the sermon on the mount (Matt. 5:1-7:29) gave us the proper interpretation of a number of the commandments. We also find in various other passages of Scripture how the writers, under the direction of the Holy Spirit, interpreted the law of God.

We need again to observe the basic principle of letting Scripture interpret Scripture in order to come to a proper understanding of the Law. For example, we might take the command "Thou shalt not kill" (Ex. 20:13, ASV) as a law against all killing, including capital punishment. When we examine Scripture in its totality however we find that God himself commanded society to take the life of anyone who has attacked the image of God by murdering another human being (Gen. 9:6). The power of the sword, which includes capital punishment, has been given to the state to enforce law and order (Rom. 13:4). So a relatively simple statement such as this commandment needs to have the full light of Scripture thrown on it if we are to understand and practice it properly.

The Concern of Sanctification

One of the great concerns that we all have as we look at ourselves is the fact that we come so far short of the standard and ultimate goal of sanctification, namely: to be perfect as the heavenly Father is perfect (Matt. 5:48). Paul seems to have been struggling with this problem himself (see Rom. 7). He says that on the one hand he delights in the law of God in his inner being (Rom. 7:22). On the other hand he finds in the members of his body a law waging war against the law of his mind (Rom. 7:23). He cries out, "What a wretched man I am! Who will rescue me from this body of death?" (Rom. 7:24).

Some see this discussion as a picture of the unconverted man prior to his coming to God, but it seems better to understand it as the Christian struggling with the remnants of sin within his nature. The natural man before regeneration does not delight in the law of God in his inner being: this can be true only of a man with a renewed heart. As he gazed at the absolute perfection of God as the standard by which he had to measure himself, Paul saw himself as "sold as a slave to sin" (Rom. 7:14). When we consider how far along the road of sanctification the apostle must have been by that time, we wonder that he viewed himself in such a low state.

The fact is, however, that when we see ourselves in light of God's perfection all of our progress is as nothing. Remember that even in later years Paul thought of himself as the chief of sinners (1 Tim. 1:15). When we look at ourselves in comparison with God we can come to no other conclusion about ourselves than that of the great yet humble apostle. We may be able to see some progress of growth in grace over the course of our Christian lives, but when we look to the absolute perfection of God we must bow before him and plead his mercy for our sins and shortcomings.

The great concern each of us should have concerning his own sanctification is the gap that remains between whatever level we may have reached and the ultimate standard of God's own perfection. Any sin that remains in the believer is a contradiction to the holiness that God has planted in us at regeneration. Whereas it is true that all our sins have been covered by the blood of Christ and that we are no longer under condemnation because Jesus has paid for each one of them, the sins the believer commits deserve the wrath and curse of God.

These remaining elements of sin in us are a total contradiction to what we are now as regenerated men and women by the grace of God. The more sanctified the believer becomes the more he will sense his failures, sins and short-comings. The more sanctified a Christian becomes the more humble he will be and the more he will recoil against any lack of conformity to the image of the son of God that he sees in himself.

Our Victory in Sanctification

As we bring this chapter to an end we need to reiterate that Jesus has gained the full victory over sin (1 Cor. 15:57). This is why Paul was able to assure us that "Sin shall not be your master, because you are not under law, but under grace" (Rom. 6:14). Therefore we are to count ourselves "dead to sin but alive to God in Christ Jesus" (Rom. 6:11). Every believer is united to Christ in his death and resurrection: he must recognize this fact and count (reckon) himself to be so united. Every believer has in Christ received victory over sin. If one does not have that victory it could be that he is not a believer. If the power of sin is not broken in a person he may not be a true believer, for when we receive Jesus Christ as Lord and Savior we are freed from the power of sin.

One final word of caution to all who are growing in grace: The basic concept of sanctification set forth in this chapter is that it is a progressive development involving a lifetime of dying more and more to sin and of living more and more to righteousness. We must never assume that, having attained a certain level in our sanctification, we will never again be in danger of falling back into deep sin. Paul warned us: "If you think you are standing firm, be careful that you don't fall!" (1 Cor. 10:12).

David is the classic example of a man who had made much progress in sanctification but fell deeply into sin. Peter also, who had been with Jesus for some three years, thought more highly of himself then he should have. The marvel of God's grace is that both men were restored to fellowship with God despite their awful sins. This gracious forgiveness should be a great comfort to each of us on those occasions when we fall into sin. Let us learn from David's psalms how to repent (see Pss. 32, 38 and 51).

Review Questions

1. What is sanctification?
2. How are justification and sanctification related?
3. What are some of the false views of sanctification? Why are they false?
4. What is the biblical teaching on sanctification? How would you share this teaching with your own children or with a new Christian?
5. What concern should each of us have about his own sanctification?
6. What kind of victory over sin do we have in Christ?

Discussion Questions

1. When Paul speaks of the Corinthians as carnal ("worldly," NIV) is he teaching that there are two classes of Christians—carnal and spiritual? Why? (See 1 Cor. 2:10-3:4.)
2. Is the idea of living a victorious Christian life biblical? Why or why not?

3. Should we "let go and let God" do our Christian living? Why or why not?
4. What would be an ideal sanctification process?
5. How can a Christian who has made much progress in sanctification fall deeply into sin?

10

THE MEANS OF GRACE TO SPIRITUAL GROWTH

Scripture Readings: Psalm 119:9-16, 105-112, Luke 11:1-13; 1 Corinthians 11:23-31

We have seen that God wants his children to grow to maturity and has provided the Holy Spirit to assist us in our sanctification. The standard by which we measure our growth and our good works is the law of God. We also noted that we are still carrying something of the old sinful nature in us and that even our best works are marred with sin. In this chapter we want to look at the aids God has graciously provided for us that we may grow more effectively. We call these aids "the means of grace."

The means of grace have been given to and should be utilized by every Christian. They are not extraordinary gifts parceled out to a few individuals but rather are special means for growth that each Christian, under ordinary circumstances, has available to him. We use the phrase *under ordinary circumstances* to remind us of the fact that in times of persecution we may not have access to some of these means. Christians in Communist lands, for example, are often deprived of the privileges of public worship and owning a Bible.

As we begin our study of the means of grace we will be considering the word of God, prayer and the two sacraments, all of which are to be used in the worship of our majestic sovereign God. Let us begin by examining the importance of worship.

Worship

As believers we respond positively to the so-great salvation God has given us by committing ourselves to worship him and by seeking to glorify him in all that we are and do. In a sense all of life for the Christian could be described as worship. Generally however we speak of worship when a believer, alone or in company with others, comes before God for the specific purpose of communing with him, praising him, and glorifying him.

We must distinguish between private and public worship. Public worship takes place when a congregation of God's covenant people gather together for the specific purpose of worship. Private worship, on the other hand, occurs when an individual believer engages in adoration and worship of God. Both kinds of worship are vital for a growing Christian life. When we neglect either of these, spiritual growth slows.

In a day and age when there is a strong emphasis on individualism, a serious problem has arisen: public or corporate worship has become relatively unimportant to some Christians. There are those who think they have done enough for God and for themselves if they have watched a worship service on television. Individuals in their homes can certainly be richly blessed by such services, but they cannot allow them to take the place of the congregational worship in which a group of individuals corporately worship the Lord.

God himself called for such public worship on a number of occasions in the Old Testament. Early in the history of Israel he required all of the people to meet together before him at the foot of Mount Sinai on the occasion of the giving of the Law (Ex. 19-24). This was the first great general assembly of God's people. The writer to the Hebrews refers back to it and indicates that we in the New Testament era have come to Mount Zion for worship. Here we meet with God, the angels and Jesus the mediator of the new covenant (Heb. 12:18-29) as a preview of that great day in heaven in which all of creation will gather before the throne of God to praise and worship him (see Rev. 4, 5).

Since God is the one who calls us to worship, he is also the one who prescribes how we are to worship. We ought to worship him only as he has directed in the word, and not according to our own imagination or desires.

The conclusion of this passage calls on all Christians to "be thankful, and so worship God acceptably with reverence and awe" (Heb. 12:28). Earlier the writer had said clearly that we must not neglect the assembling of ourselves together in worship (Heb. 10:25).

The Word

The word of God has long been recognized by most evangelical Protestants as the most important means of grace: we cannot grow spiritually without it. It is at the heart of our public worship and must be at the core of our personal devotions. It is the means by which we progress in our sanctification as the Spirit of God uses the word of God to help us grow.

God speaks to us primarily through his word, which we call the Scriptures. God has graciously given us that word in a written, objective form so that we can always have it with us. In order for us to receive a blessing from the use of the Bible and grow spiritually we should hear it with anticipation and read it with care and diligence, praying that God would open its truths to us. We must study it in a systematic way and memorize it in order to be effective in our daily lives.

We are to hear the word of God as it is preached by faithful ministers of the gospel. Historically Protestant worship services have always been Bible-centered, with the faithful proclamation of the word occupying perhaps half the time. As Christians committed to spiritual growth we must listen with anticipation, expecting a blessing and applying what we hear to our personal and family lives.

We are to commit ourselves to a regular reading of the word of God individually and as families. This consistent daily diet of the Scriptures will build fellowship with our God and put strength into our spiritual lives. It should not be a haphazard reading in which we open our Bible and blindly place a finger on a verse for that day. God can bless any reading of his word, but this is not the most profitable way in which to grow in our knowledge of the truth.

Christians should plan on reading through the whole Bible periodically. This will obviously take time, but we should allot sufficient time for our Bible reading in order to learn large portions of the text. It is most helpful, for example, to read through the shorter books of the Bible at one sitting, particularly the letters of the New Testament.

In addition to a broad reading of the Bible we need to study particular books and topics more carefully. For example, a study of the Gospels gives us a knowledge of what Jesus said and did while on earth. A study of epistles such as Romans and Galatians will give us a clearer understanding of the doctrine of justification by faith, while a study of John's first epistle will give us the assurance we need that we know God and have received the gospel.

The systematic study of a portion of Scripture requires using a notebook to outline passages and record insights that will help us grow in grace. A topical study will trace through Scripture the important themes and doctrines that may be found in the totality of the word of God; this can be done "from scratch" with the help of a concordance or through the use of a study book such as this one. Bible study enables us to compare Scripture with Scripture and to grow in our knowledge of the word, thus making us more useful in our church and more effective in our witness to the world. A variety of Bible study guides and suggestions for inductive (directly from Scripture) personal study are available on the market today. In interpreting what we study we should try to understand the context of each passage, then what the writer is trying to say in that context. This is called the grammatical-historical method of interpreting the Bible.

We should also memorize the word of God, for that makes us effective in resisting temptations, making godly decisions during the day when the Bible may not be available to us and witnessing to those who do not know Christ. Meditation on the word which we have heard, read, studied, and memorized builds greater understanding and enhances spiritual growth.

We must not stop with the intake of the word of God but must commit ourselves to apply it to our personal lives by being doers of the word as well (see Jas. 1:22). The worst critics of the Bible are not necessarily those who have intellectual problems with certain parts of it and question its validity or attack it directly: sometimes Scripture's worst enemies are those who profess to believe it but do not live by it. To grow in grace is not just to become a Bible-believer and a Bible student but to become a man or woman who applies the word regularly and seeks to live faithfully and consistently by its teachings.

In his providence and in his wisdom God has ordained that through the foolishness of preaching the gospel will be proclaimed so that the lost would be saved (1 Cor. 1:21-25) and believers edified (Rom. 1:16). We should recognize therefore the importance of being in church regularly for the preaching of the word. It is God's ordained means of spreading the word to the lost and of strengthening his church.

Prayer

As we think about communing with God we should remember that such fellowship must be two-way — that is, God speaks to us through his word and we speak to him through prayer. Prayer is the means by which we praise him for who he is and ask him for things agreeable to his will, all in the name of Jesus Christ (John 16:24).

Someone may ask, Why should we pray? We pray because God has commanded us to do so (Luke 11:9; 18:1, Eph. 6:18; 1 Thess. 5:17, 18) and he wants us to talk with him. Furthermore he is pleased to answer our prayers, though sometimes he will answer with a no for our good. We miss a tremendous blessing when we neglect to talk to God about our every need, want and desire.

The disciples on one occasion asked Jesus to teach them to pray (Luke 11:1). It is interesting to note that they did not ask Jesus to teach them how to witness or how to preach. Evidently they felt, as many of us do, that prayer is difficult and they expected the Master-teacher to instruct them. Jesus graciously granted their request and taught them what has traditionally been called the Lord's Prayer (Luke 11:2-4; see also Matt. 6:9-13). He also took many other opportunities during his short ministry to teach his disciples on the subject of prayer.

From the Lord's Prayer — really the disciple's prayer — and from Paul's teaching (1 Tim. 2:1-4) we learn that our prayers should include adoration, confession, thanksgiving and supplication both for ourselves (petition) and for others (intercession). This spells the acrostic A-C-T-S and serves as a practical reminder of the pattern for our praying. Furthermore, the Book of Psalms also gives us many examples of how we are to pray. Finally, the many recorded prayers of individuals throughout Scripture also serve as models for us on how we should pray (see Job 40:3, 4; 1 Chron. 29:10-13; 2 Chron. 6:12-42, Dan. 9:3-19, and particularly Neh. 1:5-11 as a pattern for prayer).

The Sacraments

In addition to the word and prayer, God has given us the sacraments as means of grace by which he reveals the gospel to us in what have been called "sensible signs." What God has given us in the sacraments is a way of illustrating the word to the whole man, and we see this most clearly in connection with the Lord's Supper. This sacrament is to be observed only in connection with a preaching of the word, so hearing is necessary; the elements are visible to the eye and they may also be felt, tasted and even smelled. So all five of our senses are addressed by the Lord's Supper. Baptism of course addresses the ear, the eye and the sense of touch, but not so directly the senses of taste or smell.

The sacraments are viewed in evangelical Protestantism as an extension of the preached word and in Reformed circles have been designated signs and seals of the covenant of grace. The outward signs (bread, wine, water) point to something that is signified as an internal spiritual reality (see below for each of the sacraments).

When a seal is placed on a document it serves to confirm to us the authority of that document. The sacraments do not convey to us a new or different message from that which is preached but seal or affirm to us certain spiritual realities of which we need to be reminded. They illustrate, with signs addressed to our various senses, the gospel which is preached from the word, and seal to us the promises of that gospel through our participation in the sacraments actually and personally.

Protestants generally define the sacraments as ordinances instituted by Christ for the purpose of revealing himself and the benefits of the gospel to us. By limiting the sacraments to the specific ordinances instituted by Christ we exclude from that category any of the additional ordinances observed as sacraments by the Roman Catholic Church, namely: confirmation, penance, marriage, holy orders and extreme unction. Marriage and ordination are Biblical ordinances, but they do not meet the above definition of a sacrament. A careful study of the gospel narratives reveals only two ordinances that Christ himself instituted to illustrate the gospel itself, namely: baptism (Matt. 28:19, 20) and the Lord's Supper (Matt. 26:26-30).

Baptism

Baptism is the initiatory rite by which a person is received into the visible church and the sign of our being ingrafted into Christ. In the Old Testament God commanded that every male was to be circumcised as a sign of the covenantal relationship. This was done to infants of eight days as well as to adults (Gen. 17:12). God thus included infants in the covenant community along with their parents. It was a physical sign of an internal cleansing, symbolizing circumcision of the heart.

Paul speaks of the circumcision of Christ as baptism (Col. 2:11, 12). Since the church is the continuation of God's covenant people the children of believers are to be viewed as covenant children and are to receive baptism, which has replaced circumcision. Approximately one-fourth of all the cases of Christian baptism recorded in the New Testament refer to household baptisms. No doubt these allude to the inclusion of children.

Baptism is also a ceremonial cleansing wherein, through the washing with water, we picture the cleansing that comes to believers as they come under the blood of Christ. This cleansing of course is the work of the Holy Spirit, who gives us new hearts through "the washing of regeneration" (Titus 3:5). We do not believe that water baptism saves, but we do believe that it pictures the work of the Spirit as he applies the redemption accomplished by Christ to each of our hearts. Those who have been thus cleansed by the Spirit are counted as having been ingrafted into

Christ and have the rights and privileges of membership in the church, the body of Christ.

Baptism as an initiation ceremony takes place only once. It is not to be repeated.

The Lord's Supper

The Lord's Supper, which pictures our feeding on Christ, is by Christ's command to be repeated throughout the lifetime of the believer.

Jesus himself instituted the Supper so that we would remember him and his death for us on the cross. He took from the Passover table not a portion of the lamb but a *piece of bread* and *the cup*. These two elements involve no bloodshed since they commemorate the death of Christ, the final sacrifice. So they testify to us the completed work of Christ.

It is striking to realize that, though the life and the resurrection of Christ are vital elements of our salvation, he points to his *death* in this memorial. This no doubt is due to the fact that his death is the most amazing aspect of his work. It is not too surprising that Jesus lived a perfect life of obedience and that he rose from the dead (he was the God-man, after all). But what *is* amazing is that the Prince of life would die.

The essence of the good news of the gospel is that Jesus Christ died for sinners; this is what we observe and celebrate in the Lord's Supper.

Various views have arisen in the church about the meaning of the sacrament with reference to the presence of Christ in it. One view includes the idea that the elements change their substance and actually become the very body and blood of Christ ("transubstantiation"). This is the position of the Roman Catholic Church, in which the communion table is called an altar because it is seen as a place of sacrifice.

Lutherans believe that the body and blood of Christ are actually present by, with and under the elements ("consubstantiation"). So for Luther everyone who receives the bread and wine in the mouth also receives the body and blood of Christ in the mouth.

Zwingli, the Swiss Reformer, maintained that the Lord's Supper is just a memorial of the death of Christ. Jesus is not viewed as present in any special way at the table, and those who partake receive only the bread and the wine, remembering the absent Christ.

John Calvin held that the bread and wine remained bread and wine but that Christ was spiritually present with the partaking believer. Thus the believer receives bread and wine in the mouth and Christ in the heart. In other words, Christ is really (but spiritually) present in the Supper and we receive the blessing of feeding on him as the Spirit applies him to our hearts when we observe the Supper in conformity with his word. In this way the sacrament seals to the believer the great love of Christ revealed in his self-surrender to a bitter and shameful death.

As we conclude this chapter we should examine ourselves to make sure that we are regularly and faithfully using the means of grace to grow spiritually and progress in our sanctification. Are we appropriating the word of God consistently by all means possible? Do we take our needs to God in prayer? Are we regular in our attendance upon the sacraments? Do we partake of the Lord's Supper with penitent hearts? Are we being conformed to the image of Christ, God's Son? (Rom. 8:29).

Review Questions

1. What are the means of grace?
2. What is the essence of worship?
3. How can we use the word to grow in grace?
4. Why do we pray? How do we pray?
5. What is a sacrament?
6. What is the significance of baptism? Who should be baptized? How?
7. How is the Lord present in the Lord's Supper?

Discussion Questions

1. What do you do in your private devotions? What do you read? How do you pray?
2. What is your plan for ongoing personal, applicatory Bible study?
3. What plan do you use to memorize Scripture?
4. What book of the Bible could be used as a guidebook for prayer? What are some ideas that you might get from it?
5. What do you think about as you participate in the sacraments?

11

THE CHURCH IS GOD'S BELOVED PEOPLE

Scripture Readings: Ephesians 4:1-16; 1 Peter 2:4-10

The Bible clearly teaches that there is only one church that has been brought into existence by God and belongs to him; but the Bible also makes it clear that the church may be seen in two aspects — as invisible and as visible. When we receive Christ as Lord and Savior we immediately become members of his *invisible* church. But as true believers we must also identify ourselves with his people here on earth, and we do so by uniting with a congregation of believers by making a public profession of faith. If we have not previously been baptized we are initiated into the church through that sacrament as part of our visible confession of personal trust in Christ. We speak of this act as joining the *visible* church.

The church as invisible is known only to God and includes all of the elect of all the ages from the beginning to the end. The church as visible, on the other hand, consists of all who *profess* the true faith in this world, together with their children.

It is possible that some of the elect, though coming to a sure knowledge of Christ in this life, will never unite with any visible church. The thief on the cross, for example, never had the opportunity to be baptized or received into a visible congregation of God's people. On the other hand it is possible for some to make a public profession of faith (thus joining the visible church) who really did not mean it — had never genuinely believed in Christ as Lord and Savior. Simon the sorcerer for example was baptized and received into the church in Samaria (Acts 8:13), but when he tried to buy the ability to dispense the Holy Spirit Peter said, "You have no part or share of this ministry, because your heart is not right before God" (Acts 8:21). And so Simon was for a time a member of the visible church but not of the invisible church.

This situation will exist until the consummation, since God has entrusted to fallible men who cannot look into the hearts of their fellowmen the responsibility of accepting a credible profession of faith for admission into the visible church. Ultimately, after Christ comes again and separates the sheep from the goats (see Matt. 25:31-46), the visible and invisible churches will be one and the same.

The Church in Biblical History

What we are primarily viewing in this chapter is the church as visible. From the beginning of redemptive history God has distinguished between those who belong to him and those who are in the world. In his first redemptive statement he promised that it would be through the seed of the woman that a savior would come (Gen. 3:15). Those who believed that promise became part of "the seed of the woman" — the visible church — and so in subsequent history the lines of Seth and Cain are traced as separate lines, one of faith and one of unbelief.

It was not until Abraham, however, that one specific family was singled out from the rest of the world to become the visible people of God. In other words, the Abrahamic covenant was the formal establishment of God's people as a separate entity on this earth, with a visible seal of that covenant (circumcision) to distinguish them from the world.

This concept was developed more fully when Israel was called out of Egypt and established as a kingdom of priests before God (Ex. 19:5, 6). As we noted in the last chapter, this people was called to the first general assembly of the people of God at Mount Sinai. The writer to the Hebrews described the church of the New Testament as the fulfillment of that first gathering, for today we have come to "the general assembly and church of the firstborn, which are written in heaven" (Heb. 12:23, KJV).

Some today want to make a sharp disjunction between Israel of the Old Testament and the church of the New Testament, but the unity of the people of God of all the ages makes that an invalid distinction. The Bible teaches that all of God's people are one throughout all dispensations and that the New Testament church is really a continuation of the Abrahamic covenant.

On the Day of Pentecost the apostle Peter concluded his sermon with the affirmation that the promise of the Holy Spirit is "for you and your children and for all who are far off — for all whom the Lord our God will call" (Acts 2:39). This reference to the promise of blessing goes back to Genesis 17:7 where God said he would be a God to Abraham and to his seed (true believers in God as Abraham was) after him. This was the foundation of the biblical religion of the Old Testament. Peter referred to the promise in this context when he declared that the coming of the Messiah — and subsequently of the Holy Spirit — is the fulfillment and continuation of that which had begun in the Abrahamic covenant.

Paul in writing to the Galatians made the point that Abraham is the father of the faithful of all the ages: "Understand, then, that those who believe are children of Abraham" (Gal. 3:7). In other words, Abraham is viewed as the father of all who receive the gospel by faith. He went on to make the case explicit by saying, "Christ redeemed us from the curse of the law . . . that the blessing given to Abraham might come to the Gentiles through Christ Jesus, so that by faith we might receive the promise of the Spirit" (Gal. 3:13, 14).

He went on to say, "If you belong to Christ, then you are Abraham's seed, and heirs according to the promise" (Gal. 3:29). Paul is certainly teaching the unity of the New Testament Church with Abraham's seed, the Israel of old. This is why the church of the New Testament era has sometimes been designated the New Covenant Israel.

Some New Testament Descriptions of the Church

The New Testament presents us with a number of interesting figures for the church. First, we see the church described as the body of Christ (Eph. 1:23; 2:16; 4:4; 1 Cor. 10:17). The apostle Paul portrays Jesus Christ as the head of the body (Eph. 1:23) and shows the importance of all the different parts of the body working together, each being necessary for its particular function (see 1 Cor. 12:12-27).

Second, Paul speaks of the relation of the church to Christ as that of a bride to her husband. As such she is to be submissive to him in all things (Eph. 5:22-33), and this figure becomes the basis for a glorious scene when the church is gathered to Christ and the marriage feast of the Lamb is celebrated (Rev. 19:6-9).

Third, the church is called the temple of the Lord (Eph. 2:19-22; 1 Pet. 2:5). Each stone is placed in the building just where it is needed, with Christ being the builder of this temple (Matt. 16:18, Zech. 6:12, 13).

The fourth and fifth descriptive phrases of the church are that it is the house of God—an idea similar to that of the temple of the Lord—and the pillar and ground of the truth (1 Tim. 3:15). These figures are taken from the structure of an ancient building with pillars and a foundation. The church as the pillar of the truth is to hold forth God's word to the world and build all her teachings on the foundation of that truth so as to be a sure foundation for her members.

The final phrase we want to note is one in which the people of God are described as "the church of the living God" (1 Tim. 3:15). The English word *church* is derived from a Greek word meaning "the Lord's" and is used to translate another Greek term which means the "called-out ones" or "the assembly." Those who have been called into a saving relationship belong to the one who is the true, only and living God.

The Keys of the Kingdom

The Bible presents Christ as the Lord of his church. Jesus indicated this when he responded to Peter's great confession of faith and declared, "On this rock I will build my church" (Matt. 16:18). He then spoke of the keys of the kingdom of heaven and indicated that the disciples would be granted authority on earth to bind and to loose (16:19). This authority was again referred to in Matthew 18:18 when Jesus described how we ought to deal with an erring brother. We should first go to him, and if he will not hear us we must go again with witnesses; if he still refuses to deal with his sin the matter is to be taken to the whole church.

It is at this point that Jesus said, "Again, I tell you that if two of you on earth agree about anything you ask for, it will be done for you by my Father in heaven" (Mt. 18:19). This is significant in that it indicates that whenever the church exercises discipline it does so with the authority of heaven itself, when it is done in accord with the word. Jesus again said essentially the same thing in the upper room after the resurrection as he gave his Spirit to the disciples (John 20:22, 23). This marked the official conveyance of his authority and power to the church. It is a power that continues to reside in the church visible.

The source of this power is the Lord Jesus Christ, who is the head of the church and has authority in heaven and on earth. The nature of this power is spiritual—that is, it is in the realm of spiritual sanctions only. This authority is exercised as the church admits persons to membership in the visible church, and as necessary excludes others.

The only lawbook the church has is the word of God, and the church's task is not to make laws but to declare what God has already given us in his written word. In other words, the church's function is not legislative but declarative. This is true of the formulating of confessions, catechisms, creeds and books of church order as well as judicial decisions. When these things are faithfully done in conformity with the word, the visible church is functioning biblically and her leaders and declarative statements are to be obeyed.

The Marks of the Church

Because of the many different churches that exist today we need to have some standards by which to determine whether a particular church is a true church or not. The Reformers set forth three basic marks of the true church: the sound proclamation of the word, the true administration of the sacraments and the proper exercise of discipline. The first of these actually encompasses the second and third, for where there is a full commitment in the church to the word and to its sound proclamation there will of necessity be the proper administration of the sacraments and the true exercise of discipline. When a church ceases to do either of the latter two it has in effect already abandoned the first of these marks of the true church.

The Government of the Church

Certain basic principles of church government may be found in Scripture. First, we note that the apostles did not assert their authority in naming their own successors or other officers of the church. In fact, when faced with the need for assistance in the temporal affairs of the church, they directed the congregation to choose seven godly men to serve in this capacity. After the choice was made the apostles set these deacons apart with prayer and with the laying on of hands, which is now called ordination (Acts 6:1-6).

As Paul and Barnabas were leaving the churches they had established on their first missionary journey they appointed elders in each of the congregations (Acts 14:23). From this and other passages we deduce that there was a plurality of elders in each congregation (Acts 20:17, Phil. 1:1, Titus 1:5). The idea of elders in every congregation was not new with Paul, for this is how every synagogue was governed. The church simply borrowed the Jewish system that had been developed in the Old Testament.

With the rule of elders in the local congregations the early church also developed the use of a graduated court system. We can discern this from the fact that when a problem arose in Antioch of Syria the church there sent representatives to the apostles and elders in Jerusalem, who after a considerable debate decided the issue and circulated their decision among the churches (see Acts 15:1-35).

From this brief survey of some of the New Testament passages that indicate the form that church government took in the apostolic age we derive the system known today as the presbyterian form of government. The word comes from the Greek term for "elder" (presbyterian) and describes the type of church government in which elders elected by the congregation rule the body of God's people as their servant-leaders in the decision-making process. The graduated court system mentioned above extends this congregational form to the regional body we call the presbytery and the national (or international) form we designate as the general assembly.

Though this system of church government is in closest conformity with Scripture, belief in it or practice of it is not essential to the existence of a church. In other words, if a church has another form of government it does not mean that it is not a true church. Biblical church government is not necessary for the being of the church, but it is necessary for the well-being of the church. We should seek however to make sure that our church is as biblical as it can possibly be, including its form of government.

The Mission of the Church

Christ as king has given to the church her mission in what we call the Great Commission (Matt. 28:19, 20). This commission has two basic tasks. The first is the evangelistic thrust by which the church of all the ages is charged to go and make disciples of all nations; the second is that of teaching those gathered into the fold "to obey everything I have commanded you" (Matt. 28:20).

We sometimes have a tendency to think only of the evangelistic aspect as the real fulfillment of this commission. A careful study of the command given by Jesus indicates a balance between the two thrusts of the commission. We are not fulfilling the great commission if we do only the evangelistic work and neglect the instruction of those who have been gathered into the church, nor are we carrying out the great commission if we only educate our people and do not reach out to disciple all nations.

This is the only commission that Jesus Christ has given to his church. Much pressure has been brought to bear on the church today to become involved in various social or political works. The church *as the church,* however, has no business doing anything other than what Jesus has commissioned her to do. If the church carries out the function of teaching all things to her members, then *Christians* will carry into the various areas of life the Christian ethic.

When Jesus gave the Great Commission he based it on the fact that he claimed authority over every area of life (see Matt. 28:18). The church should recognize this kingship of Christ over all of life and instruct its members how they should behave in various spheres of societal living, and then Christians should carry out these principles in all their contacts within society. They do this as individuals or perhaps in association with other Christians in voluntary organizations such as school societies, political action groups and helping to feed starving people — but not as the church.

Unity and Diversity in the Church

The early church established a number of different congregations. As we consider how many souls were converted on the Day of Pentecost and shortly thereafter (see Acts 2:41; 4:4; 6:7) we may deduce that this large body did not meet in one location. The church had various congregations throughout Jerusalem just as the Jews had many synagogues in the city. When Paul talks about the church in Jerusalem he is speaking of this group of smaller congregations which constituted the church in that city. The same would be true of his reference to the church in Ephesus, for such a large city would also have had many congregations.

We gather from the letter to Philemon that a congregation met in his home (Philem. 2), but the same city of Colosse also had a congregation meeting in the house of Nympha (Col. 4:15). From these several references we see that the term *church* was sometimes applied to a local congregation as well as to all the congregations of a city or region. During New Testament times we do not find the church divided into denominations — this was a later development in the church's history.

The eastern and western branches of Christendom had already divided prior to the Protestant Reformation. After the Reformation there came a splintering of the western church into a number of different branches which we now call denominations. These groupings generally reflect differences in theological beliefs.

If we all understood the Bible fully and accurately there would be neither need nor excuse for such divisions in the church, but due to the sinfulness that remains in our natures we develop blind spots regarding different doctrines of the faith. The result is the fragmenting into denominations.

It is clear from the high-priestly prayer of Christ that he desires unity in the church (John 17:21-23). The kind of unity he prayed for, of course, was not a forced organizational unity in which churches would continue to have sharp theological differences. Since he mentioned the unity that he had with the Father he was certainly referring to spiritual unity, not merely organizational unity. That is the kind of unity we should seek in the church today.

The danger that those of us face who have reacted to the modern liberal ecumenical movement (which sees unity primarily in terms of organizational union) is that we will not be interested in ecumenism at all. We need to develop a biblical ecumenism and work for the union of all Christians who stand solidly on the Bible as the word of God, so that we may demonstrate the kind of unity Jesus prayed for in his great high-priestly prayer (see John 17).

Review Questions

1. How would you distinguish between the church as visible and as invisible? What does that mean to us practically?
2. What are the biblical grounds for holding the visible church in high esteem?
3. How is the visible church *one* in all the ages of biblical history?
4. What are some of the figures used to picture the church?
5. What authority does the visible church have? Why?
6. What are the marks of a true church?
7. What is the mission of the church? How is this mission to be carried out?

Discussion Questions

1. What constitutes a valid reason for leaving a particular church?
2. Why did your particular denomination form? Was it on biblical grounds?
3. Is it important to belong to a branch of the visible church? Why should you join a church? What are the disadvantages of not joining a body of believers?
4. Why do you belong to your church? What do you contribute to your church by being a member? What does your church contribute to your spiritual well-being?
5. How should the church or its members handle their concern over the issues of abortion, the possibility of nuclear war and the starvation of millions of people?

12

THE LAST THINGS

Scripture Readings: 2 Corinthians 5:1-10; 1 Thessalonians 4:13-18

The Bible tells us that all things will come to an end some day. Just as there was a definite beginning to all things (the creation) so there will be an end to all things (the consummation). Concerning "the last things" there has been much curiosity and debate through the centuries. Men always have questions about the future and try to "see" into it in some way.

What is going to happen to us when we die? If we are Christians will we go straight to heaven or do we have to go to some intermediate state or place for a while? What happens to our bodies? What is going to happen when Jesus comes again? These and many other questions are part of our natural curiosity about the future.

We need to realize however that the Bible does not give us answers to all of the questions we may ask, particularly those having to do with the future. Certain principles and some facts are given in plain language but other truths have to be gleaned from isolated passages of Scripture. Too, some of the answers are phrased in language that is difficult for us to understand, and many have been the interpretations of the details of the events of the last times among evangelical Christians who are committed to the integrity of the Scriptures.

The Bible gives us two kinds of information about the future: some passages of Scripture tell us about what happens to individuals at death and in the general resurrection; others tell us about what is going to happen to the world when Jesus returns in power and glory. We will examine some selective passages on each of these topics.

Teachings About the Individual's Future

Death and the Intermediate State

Unless Jesus Christ returns first, all of us as human beings face death, an experience that none of us has yet undergone and so a great unknown. Since it means the end of our earthly lives and involves an unexperienced future we all have a natural dread of it. It is normal for us to want to know what is going to happen when we die. It is the third of the great philosophical questions of mankind: Where am I going [after death]?

Let us begin with a biblical presentation on death. First, death was not a part of our original state. It was introduced as part of the curse after the fall of man. Originally man was made not to die but to live. Because death was part of the curse and totally foreign to our original natures even Jesus recoiled from it in the Garden of Gethsemane.

Second, the Bible teaches that death is the separation of the soul-or-spirit aspect of man from his body. We see this in reverse in passages recording a resurrection where it is said that the life or spirit returned to the body (1 Kings 17:22, Luke 8:55). This indicates that death involves the departure of the soul or spirit of man from his body. Our bodies of course remain here on earth and are buried, returning to the dust from which they were originally taken. But what happens to the soul of man?

Happily the Bible does not leave us in the dark regarding this. The apostle Paul talked about this subject in his second letter to the Corinthians. In one passage he spoke of "the earthly tent we live in" (2 Cor. 5:1). This language may seem obscure to us but the apostle made it clear later in the passage that this is a reference to the body (see 2 Cor. 5:6-9). Even believers do not wish "to be unclothed" (to die — 2 Cor. 5:2-4). We have a fear of being unclothed, and this suggests that human nature is a union of body and soul (spirit). To face the separation of these two aspects of our being is threatening to us, so we are afraid.

Christians who know that eventually they will receive glorified bodies look forward to being "clothed" again with that body (2 Cor. 5:4). Having said this Paul went on to say that while we are in our bodies here we are absent from the Lord (2 Cor. 5:6). This being the case, "to be away from the body" is to be "at home with the Lord" (2 Cor. 5:7). In other words, when we die and our souls depart from our bodies we will immediately be in the Lord's presence. We find no hint in the Bible of any stay in some intermediate state.

Paul affirmed the same thing as he looked at the possibility of his own imminent death: "For to me, to live is Christ and to die is gain" (Phil. 1:21). Obviously Paul expected some gain to accrue to him at his death; this could be the case only if he was sure of going to be with the Lord at his death.

That Christians who die go to be with Jesus is confirmed by what Paul said when he described the Lord's return, when Christ will bring with him all those who have "fallen asleep" (died) in him (1 Thess. 4:14).

The Final State of Man

We should note here that, though our souls at death go to be with the Lord Jesus, this is not to be our final state. It is sometimes spoken of as an intermediate state, a form of existence between the time we die and the final resurrection at the second coming of the Lord.

As we study carefully Paul's teaching to the Thessalonian church we learn that when Jesus returns he will bring with him those Christians who have fallen asleep in him (1 Thess. 4:14, 15). Then their old bodies will be raised as resurrection bodies and their souls will be returned to them. Only then will those who are still alive be called up. Paul teaches us that those who are alive at the time Jesus returns will not die but will in the twinkling of an eye experience a change in which their bodies will be glorified and become just like the resurrection bodies of those who had died (1 Cor. 15:52ff).

But what about non-Christians? We are not told much about them except through the story of Lazarus and the rich man (Luke 16:19-31). We note here that the souls of both believing Lazarus and the unbelieving rich man were conscious after death. Lazarus went to paradise (Abraham's bosom) whereas the rich man was in a place of torment. As in the case of believers the disembodied state of unbelievers is not their final state but an intermediate one. Whereas believers go into the presence of the Lord unbelievers immediately enter into their deserved torments.

Jesus taught that when he returns he will call all the dead out of their graves to either a resurrection of life or a resurrection of judgment (John 5:25-29). From this teaching we conclude that, just as the believers have their souls restored to their resurrected bodies, so also the wicked shall be resurrected and have their souls restored to their bodies. They will then enter into judgment in the whole man, body and soul, just as believers enter into glory in their total beings, body and soul.

The Glorious Return of Jesus Christ

The second coming has primarily to do with the return of Jesus Christ in great power and glory as well as a complex series of events that will take place in connection with it.

Bible-believing scholars have been divided in their opinions on the sequence and chronology of these events. Each of the three basic views has certain strong points and certain weak points that we should recognize. We must realize that we cannot be absolutely certain and dogmatic about future events. It is likely that no one has worked out all of the details of the prophecies exactly as they are to be fulfilled. God has chosen to give us only general statements and some principial details about future events. We shall all be surprised at what the final fulfillment will be.

Many of the differences of opinion center around the meaning of the "thousand years" in Revelation 20 and the relation of Christ's return to this millennium (Latin for "thousand years"). These viewpoints have historically been labeled with respect to Christ's coming *before* the millennium ("pre-"), *after* the millennium ("post-") or there not being a literal earthly millennium ("a-").

The Premillennial View

One of the most popular views held by many evangelical Christians today is that Christ will come back and establish his millennial kingdom. This view is called "premillennial" because it sees Christ coming back to earth *prior* to the beginning of the millennium. At his return Christ will bind Satan for a thousand years and usher in his visible thousand-year kingdom on the earth, and this period will be one of peace and great prosperity for the whole earth under the personal kingship of Jesus himself.

The millennium will end when Satan is again loosed. A final period of apostasy and rebellion will take place. Christ and his armies will defeat both Satan and the rebels to usher in the final judgment, after which the final state will begin.

The premillennial view has a number of variations which center on the issue of a tribulation period on earth prior to the millennium. One such variant, popularized by the *Scofield Reference Bible,* makes a sharp distinction between the nation of Israel and the New Testament church and sees a seven-year tribulation *before* the second coming of Christ, at the beginning of which the church (true believers in Christ) will be raptured (taken up to be with the Lord). This view also believes that the millennial kingdom is essentially Jewish in character. Some see the rebuilding of the temple in Jerusalem and the reestablishment of sacri-

ficial worship. Christ will be ruling on his throne in Jerusalem. The New Testament church is enjoying its rewards
in heaven. This view has been called "pretribulational
premillennialism" or "dispensationalism."

The historic premillennial position does not make the
sharp distinction between Israel and the church. It holds
to an indefinite tribulation period for the church before the
second coming of Christ, followed by a millennium that is
the "golden age" for all men on the earth.

Premillennialists believe that they are interpreting the
Scriptures more literally than those who hold the other
views. Those who do not accept this view believe that to
take a single passage (Rev. 20) and make it the basis on
which to build their whole view of the last times is not a
good method of biblical interpretation.

The Postmillennial View

The other two views are really postmillennial in nature,
for both teach that Christ returns *after* the millennium.
The view known as postmillennialism maintains that a
general acceptance of the gospel will take place in the
world, resulting in a prolonged golden age — perhaps a
literal thousand years — on earth.

Variations of this position differ as to how the millennium will come about. Some have seen it as taking place
with the conversion of the Jews, which in turn will bring
about a general conversion of the world. Others maintain
that it will take place after a general collapse of the world
systems and the emergence of the church with a Christian
reconstruction of law and order in the world. The historic

position has been that the preaching of the gospel itself will eventually bring about a general conversion of the world that will usher in the golden age.

At the end of the millennium Christ will return and judge the whole earth, after which the final state will begin. One of the attractive features of any form of postmillennialism is its optimism that the gospel of Christ will conquer the world. Like premillennialism it holds to a literal golden age. One of the major weak points of this view is the negation of the expectancy we have of Christ's imminent return that many passages of Scripture seem to teach. In this view Christ will not return until after a literal millennium takes place, which means that believers will not be able to look expectantly for his return until a thousand years after the millennium *begins* — and this has not yet occurred.

The Amillennial View

The third basic position is known as the amillennial (nonmillennial) view because it sees the whole present church age as the millennium in a spiritual sense. It does not hold with a period of a literal thousand years. A recent writer has suggested that a better name for this position would be "realized millennialism." The basic view is that the present period of time between the ascension of Christ and his second coming is actually a realization of the millennium in a spiritual sense.

At the end of history Christ will return and judge the whole earth, ushering in the final state. This view interprets the thousand years of Revelation 20 in a symbolic sense (inasmuch as the whole book uses so much symbolism) and interprets it in the light of the rest of Scripture rather than making it the basis of all interpretation. One of the weaknesses of this view is the difficulty in seeing how some of the optimistic prophetic passages are to be fulfilled.

Points Held in Common by All Views

Regardless of which of the three views a person holds it should be noted that all three do justice to the biblical teaching of the personal, visible and glorious return of the Lord Jesus. All three see present history culminating in the final judgment, to be followed by the eternal state — blessedness in the new heavens and the new earth for believers, punishment in hell for the wicked.

Many tend to think of the final state of blessedness for believers as our being in heaven with the Lord. A careful reading of the last two chapters of the book of Revelation, together with such passages as Isaiah 66 and 2 Peter 3, shows that the final residence of the righteous will be on the new earth. We see a picture of the descent of the new Jerusalem from heaven to earth in Revelation 21:1-5.

The new Jerusalem symbolizes the church, the bride of Christ, which is placed on the new earth. We are not told much about what we will be doing for all eternity, but from the fact that our Creator is active we may deduce that in our state of full likeness to him we too will be active in eternity. We will be able to develop on the new earth a culture that is without sin.

Even if we are not absolutely certain about the exact order of the events accompanying our Lord's return, we should all look expectantly for that return. Furthermore, though we may not be able to describe what we will be doing in eternity, we know that we shall be totally joyful in the presence of Christ, whom we will perfectly worship and adore. We will be able truly "to glorify God and to enjoy him forever" (Westminster Shorter Catechism #1).

"He who testifies to these things says, 'Yes, I am coming soon.' Amen. Come, Lord Jesus" (Rev. 22:20).

Review Questions

1. What is the nature of death? Why are we generally afraid of it?
2. What is the basic meaning of death in the Bible? What does it mean to believers and to unbelievers?
3. What does the Bible teach about the souls of believers at death?
4. How will the intermediate state end?
5. What are the advantages of each of the millennial views? What are the difficulties with each view?

Discussion Questions

1. Why must Christians go through the experience of death?
2. Where will we spend eternity? What will it be like? What is the major thing you are looking forward to in eternity?
3. How are we to be ready for Christ's coming?
4. Why has God not told us when the end will come?
5. What millennial position most appeals to you? Why?

13

THE SYSTEM OF CHRISTIAN BELIEF

When we began our study of what Christians believe we set out to answer some of the many probing theological questions that many of us have. We turned to the Bible, the only true source of knowledge for this topic, and tried to find some basic answers to a number of sometimes difficult questions. Of necessity our studies have been brief and sometimes only introductory to the various subjects we considered. As we noted in the Author's Note our hope is that this book will whet the appetite of its readers for a fuller study into the many subjects of Christian doctrine.

In this chapter we want to draw together what we have studied so that we can get an overall view of what Christian doctrine is all about. Evangelical Christians maintain that all truth comes from God, and one of the implications of this is the concept of the unity of all truth. We have studied the various divisions of theology in this book and now we should try to see how they fit together into a unified system of thought. In order to do this we will use the outline of the various heads usually treated under systematic theology, summarizing in a sentence or two the results of our studies on each topic.

Foundations: The Bible Is God's Very Word

All Scripture is God-breathed and is without error as originally given. The books belonging in the Bible were determined by the Holy Spirit, who inspired the writers; they were then recognized by the church as coming through divinely appointed spokesmen or writers.

God: God Is the Majestic Sovereign

The God of the Bible is the creator of the heavens and the earth. He is infinite, eternal and unchangeable in all his attributes. He exists in three persons — Father, Son and Holy Spirit. These three are the same in essence, equal in power and glory. This God is the Lord of heaven and earth, time and history, and has a plan that includes all that is to take place. He is the sovereign triune God.

Creation: God Is the Great Creator

God carries out his plans in three ways: his eternal decrees, the work of creation and the work of providence. God created all things in an orderly progression and sustains and governs all that he created. Man made in the image and likeness of God was the climax of this creation, and then the whole work of creation was capped with God's resting and the institution of the Sabbath.

Man: The Crown of God's Creation

Man, male and female, was made in the image of God and as originally created was righteous. Endowed with a holy nature that was subject to change, he was to function as a prophet, a priest and a king.

Sin: The Fall and Its Consequences

Adam, the first man, was placed on probation under the covenant of works. He was responsible to obey God perfectly, especially with regard to the tree of the knowledge of good and evil. Adam sinned in the eating of the forbidden fruit. In that rebellion he acted for the whole human race as its federal head, and so his sin affected all of his posterity. All mankind, descending from him by ordinary generation, sinned in him and fell with him, making themselves liable to the miseries of this life, to death and finally to hell itself.

Christ: The Person and Work of Christ

Jesus Christ is the mediator of the covenant of grace. He is the second person of the holy Trinity who voluntarily came into this world and assumed a human nature so that he could represent us as the second Adam. He is both God and man in two distinct natures while continuing to be but one person. He was born of a virgin and lived a sinless life. He carried out perfectly the three offices originally assigned to Adam:

prophet — he was the spokesman for God;

priest — he represented us to God in the sacrifice of himself on the cross for our sins;

king — he is the ruler over all things as the King of kings and Lord of lords.

Justification: The Holy Spirit Applies the Gospel of Christ to the Elect by Effectually Calling Them to Salvation.

We receive our justification only by faith, through which we rest on Christ alone for our salvation from sin. God pardons our sins and accepts us as righteous in his sight on the grounds of the righteousness of Christ, which he imputes to us when we trust in him.

Adoption: God Brings Us into His Family

He makes us heirs of eternal life and joint heirs with Jesus Christ.

Sanctification: We Grow Spiritually and Do Good Works

We are justified by faith alone, but we are responsible to produce good works. Sanctification is a process — beginning with our regeneration and continuing throughout our lives — whereby we are able to die more and more to sin and live more and more to righteousness by the power of the Holy Spirit who lives in us.

The Means of Grace: God Has Graciously Provided Means for Us to Grow in Holiness and Godliness

The means of grace are the word, prayer and the sacraments. We should make diligent use of these means so that the Lord will bless us with growth in our spiritual lives.

The Church: God Has Called Out a People for Himself

God has his own special people, who are distinguished from the world. They include believers and their children. Jesus as the king of his church has given it one primary task: to gather the elect into the body and to teach them his word. The church has spiritual authority that is exercised through its duly constituted officers. They act with Christ's authority when they do so in accord with his word.

Last Things: The Certainty of the Future

The souls of individual believers at death go immediately into the presence of Christ. Their bodies remain in the grave until the resurrection of the dead at the return of the Lord Jesus. The sequence of the events that take place at the return of Christ has been subjected to a variety of interpretations by believing scholars. The three basic positions are premillennialism (Christ comes again before the millennium), postmillennialism (Christ comes to earth after the millennium), and amillennialism (the millennium is the present age in symbolic form). Regardless of the millennial view we may hold, all of us need to be looking for the personal return of Christ.

Having thus seen the system of Christian doctrine as a whole we need to pause to consider the proper place of such an arrangement. If there was ever an appropriate system of thought that could be considered worthy of studying for its own sake, it would be theology. But if we stop here we have missed the whole point of Christian thought, for as we study the Bible we find that unless we come to recognize our need as sinners for a Redeemer, and unless we come to find Jesus as the only all-sufficient Savior, we have completely misunderstood the purpose of the Scripture and of theology.

The ultimate purpose of theology is to lead us to practice godliness, to lead the kind of meaningful lives God wants us to have. If our study in this area results only in speculative considerations and does not bring about change for the better in our lives, we will not have fulfilled the purpose of the study.

With privileges come responsibilities. With the privilege of having gained further or new knowledge of what God requires of us comes the responsibility of *doing* — living the way God wants us to live and doing the good works he wants us to do. So each one of us is called to certain responses to each of the doctrines we have studied in this book.

Several passages of Scripture deal specifically with this necessary response. The first required response is for us to believe the gospel, believe in Christ and receive him as Lord and Savior (if we have not already done so). Paul and Silas answered the question of the Philippian jailer about how to be saved by saying, "Believe in the Lord Jesus, and you will be saved — you and your household" (Acts 16:31). Note that this involves faith — the placing of trust in Christ. The apostles did not say to believe *about* Jesus but to believe *in* him. Then and now we are called to put our total trust in him as our Lord and Savior.

Included in the transaction of receiving Christ as Lord and Savior is the necessity of our being serious about turning from our sins, which the Bible calls repentance. Peter ended his Day-of-Pentecost sermon with the following invitation: "Repent and be baptized, every one of you, in the name of Jesus Christ so that your sins may be forgiven" (Acts 2:38). In his sermon at Athens Paul declared, "But now he [God] commands all people everywhere to repent" (Acts 17:30).

If we should say that the doctrine of predestination (election) excuses us from responding to the gospel then we need to hear again the invitation that Jesus gave after thanking God for that very doctrine. "Come to me, all you who are weary and burdened, and I will give you rest. Take my yoke upon you and learn from me, for I am gentle and humble in heart, and you will find rest for your souls. For my yoke is easy and my burden is light" (Matt. 11:28-30). Jesus lays the responsibility for coming to him on us.

For those of us who have already received Christ as Lord and Savior and know Jesus personally this book should become a stimulus for growth in grace. The Bible exhorts us often to live more-godly lives, to walk in intimacy with the Lord and to be holy. Listen to Jesus in his call to discipleship. "If you love me, you will obey what I command" (John 14:15). Here he gives us a means to demonstrate our love for him, namely: to obey what he has commanded.

Jesus returned to this theme time and again in this last discourse to his disciples before his death. "If you obey my commands, you will remain in my love, just as I have obeyed my Father's commands and remain in his love . . . My command is this: Love each other as I have loved you . . . This is my command: Love each other" (John 15:10, 12, 17). We are to obey God's commandments as an evidence of our love for him. In particular we are commanded to love each other as he has loved us. We do that best when we are growing spiritually, walking daily with Jesus Christ, doing our part to progress toward godliness and holiness and doing the good works to which we have been foreordained (Eph. 2:10). This book was written to help us meet these objectives.

Review Questions

1. What do you believe about the Bible? What difference should that make in your life?
2. What do you believe about the Trinity? What difference should that make in your life?
3. What do you believe about man? What difference should that make in your life?
4. What do you believe about sin? What difference should that make in your life?
5. What do you believe about Jesus Christ? What difference should that make in your life?
6. What do you believe about the accomplishment of your salvation by Christ? What difference should that make in your life?
7. What do you believe about the application of your salvation by the Holy Spirit? What difference should that make in your life?
8. What benefits result from receiving Christ as Lord and Savior? What difference should that make in your life?
9. What do you believe about the means of grace? What difference should that make in your life?
10. What do you believe will happen at the end of time? What difference should that make in your life?
11. What response have you made or do you choose to make to the system of Christian belief discussed in this book? What difference should that make in your life?
12. Where do you go from here?